Also by JONATHAN YARDLEY

OUR KIND OF PEOPLE: *The Story of an American Family*

RING: *A Biography of Ring Lardner*

Out of Step

Out of Step

Notes from a Purple Decade

by Jonathan Yardley

Villard Books / New York / 1991

Grateful acknowledgment is made to the following for permission to reprint previously published material:

THE AMERICAN SCHOLAR: Excerpts from "A Decent Impersonality" by Christopher Clausen from *The American Scholar,* Volume 54, Number 4, Autumn 1985. Copyright © 1985 by the author. By permission of the publishers.

MICHAEL IMISON PLAYWRIGHTS LTD. and WARNER/CHAPPELL MUSIC, INC.: Excerpt from Noël Coward's version of "Let's Do It (Let's Fall in Love)" by Cole Porter. Noël Coward's lyrics copyright © Estate of Noël Coward. Cole Porter's lyrics copyright 1928 Warner Bros. Inc. (Copyright renewed.) All rights reserved. Reprinted by arrangement with Michael Imison Playwrights Ltd. and Warner/Chappell Music, Inc.

THE NEW YORK TIMES COMPANY: Excerpts from "The Lasting Power of the Political Novel" by Mary McCarthy; "Endowment Suspends Grants for Art Critics" by Grace Glueck; "U.S. Literature Canon Under Siege" by Joseph Berger; a review by Benjamin DeMott; a January 24, 1988, article in *The New York Times Book Review,* and a May 5, 1988, article about the auctioning of a Saul Bellow manuscript. Copyright © 1984, 1988 by The New York Times Company. Reprinted by permission.

PUBLISHERS WEEKLY and ROBERT WARD: Excerpts from "Sensibility and the Novel" by Robert Ward reprinted from the April 5, 1985, issue of *Publishers Weekly,* published by R. R. Bowker Company, a Xerox Company. Copyright © 1985 by Xerox Corporation.

U.S. TRUST AND COMPANY: Excerpt from *Selected Letters of John O'Hara* edited by Matthew Bruccoli. Reprinted by permission of U.S. Trust and Company as Executor of the Will of John O'Hara.

THE WALL STREET JOURNAL: Excerpts from "That Tuition Check May Pay for a Course About Rock and Roll" by Eugene Carlson. Copyright © 1988 by Dow Jones & Company, Inc. All rights reserved worldwide. Reprinted by permission of *The Wall Street Journal.*

WARNER/CHAPPELL MUSIC, INC.: Excerpts from "Bewitched, Bothered and Bewildered" by Lorenz Hart and Richard Rodgers. Copyright 1951 by Chappell & Co. (renewed). All rights reserved. Used by permission.

THE WASHINGTON POST COMPANY: Excerpts from "That's a Classic?" Copyright © 1983 by The Washington Post Co. Reprinted with permission.

Library of Congress Cataloging-in-Publication Data

Yardley, Jonathan.

Out of step/by Jonathan Yardley.
p. cm.
Originally published in the Washington Post.
ISBN 0-394-58910-6
1. Books—Reviews. I. Title.
Z1035.A1Y28 1991
028.1—dc20 90-36283

Designed by Anita Karl and Jim Kemp
Manufactured in the United States of America
9 8 7 6 5 4 3 2

FIRST EDITION

For Sue

constant reader

Preface

When old newspaper pieces find new life between the covers of books, their authors seem duty bound to apologize for the temerity of the enterprise; such collections are assumed to be acts of immodesty and futility—the embalming of yesterday's stale news—and no doubt there's an element of truth to the assumption. But you'll find no such apologies herein. For as long as I can remember I have loved collections of other people's work—heaven knows there are plenty of them on my bookshelves—and I am delighted to have the opportunity to issue one of my own. I have no illusions about the merits of these pieces either collectively or individually, and I'll be the first to admit that all of them have their origins in passing events that are by now quite thoroughly past; yet most of them seem to me to deal with larger issues that transcend topicality, and for better or worse all of them speak quite clearly in my own voice.

They cover nearly ten years, from the fall of 1981 to December of 1989. In 1981, I went to work for the *Washington Post* as its book critic, but as it is in the nature of newspapers both large and small to insist that book reviewing is not a full-time job, I soon found myself doing something else: writing a column that appeared each Monday morning in the *Post*'s much-celebrated (and much-denigrated) soft-news potpourri, the "Style" section. It took awhile for the column to find its niche, but gradually it evolved into a place for commentary on issues not often addressed in newspaper opinion sections: cultural and literary affairs, education both higher and lower, the press and the media, the ebb and flow of American social life. In a newspaper where politics is the food of news I chose to eschew it, though as you will see from time to time I found its temptations irresistible.

Thus the column continues now, as presumably it will until it, and I, wear down. The pieces I have chosen to assemble herein are accurately representative of what I write about and how I write about it, though with certain exceptions. The life of a columnist is like any other in that it involves a lot of routine business that, once discharged, is of no further interest. For a while, for example, I wrote a fair amount about the shabby treatment of authors in the Tax Reform Act of 1986; the pieces may have been useful in a good cause, and I'm glad I wrote them, but the issue is dead. I wrote even more about the controversies of William J. Bennett during his tenure at the Department of Education—I was his sympathizer, though scarcely his partisan—but that too is yesterday's news. The scandalous state of big-time college athletics has been a subject of greater concern to me than the single piece in this book might indicate, but one selection seemed sufficient.

The subjects about which I write divide themselves naturally into the two broad categories in which most of this book has been organized. Early in the life of the column I discovered that as a practicing book reviewer, I found it a great luxury to have a forum in which to discuss literary and book-industry matters that transcend a book reviewer's business; thus the book's first section, my little valentine to the reigning gods and goddesses of what passed for serious literature in the America of the eighties. I further found it wonderfully gratifying to have a place in which to write about matters that eluded me as a book reviewer, since my obligation in that capacity is to pass judgment on individual books rather than to use them as springboards for my opinions on other issues; thus the book's second section, where I rattle on in many directions about life in America during the late, and by me most passionately unlamented, reign of Ronald Reagan. As to the book's third section, it is a postscript but one of which I am fond: a few pieces of a personal, though I pray not narcissistic, nature.

The pieces are arranged chronologically within each section; there seemed no good reason to impose any artificial thematic organization upon them and, as it turned out, from time to time the chronological setting produced apt if accidental juxtapositions. The columns appear largely, but not entirely, as they did originally. I have tried to eradicate repetition where it was especially blatant, and I have been unable to resist the temptation to polish my prose, but no opinions have been revised and in instances where I subsequently was proved wrong, the error is there for all to see.

THE PUBLICATION of a book such as this provides an opportunity to say thanks, and I herewith seize it. Though this book covers only my years at the *Washington Post,* what I did in those years is the summary of all that went before. My thanks stretch back to 1961, when I left the University of North Carolina and began my life as a man.

At the *New York Times,* where I worked from 1961 to 1964: James Reston (for more about him, see page 257), Wallace Carroll and the late John Desmond.

At the *Greensboro Daily News,* 1964 to 1974: William D. Snider, the late James Ross and the late H. W. Kendall.

At the *Miami Herald,* 1974 to 1978: Larry Jinks, Jay Clarke and Ron Martin.

At the *Washington Star,* 1978 to 1981: Jeffrey Frank and Jack Schnedler.

At the *Washington Post:* Ednamae Storti, Brigitte Weeks, Alice Digilio, Nina King, Michael Dirda, Reid Beddow, David Nicholson, Francis Tanabe, Shelby Coffey, Mary Hadar, Jill Grisco, Richard Harwood, Peter Silberman, Robert Kaiser, Leonard Downie, Benjamin Bradlee and Donald Graham.

At other points of my compass: Reed Whittemore, Robert Creamer, Barbara LaFontaine, Pat Ryan, J. Anthony Lukas,

Robert D. Loomis, Dan Green, Liz Darhansoff and, most recently, Peter Gethers.

Two names are missing and now to be accounted for. At the *Greensboro Daily News* from 1965 to 1974, then again at the *Washington Star* from 1978 to 1981, I worked with Edwin M. Yoder, Jr., more closely, happily and rewardingly than I have worked with anyone at any place; his influence upon me is as incalculable as it is generous, he is the reader whom I see in my mind when I write, and he is therefore to be held responsible for every word in this book. At the *Miami Herald* from 1975 to 1978 and at the *Washington Post* from 1981 to, I hope, the day I retire, I have worked with Ellen Edwards, my cherished friend and irreplaceable editor; she's responsible for this stuff, too. To have had two such colleagues as these is, I think, as much as anyone rightfully can hope for or deserve.

The last word is for my wife. This book is dedicated to her, with two words that begin, if only begin, to describe her utterly essential role in my life. The rest of the story is, as it should be, between the two of us.

Contents

PART ONE: THE LIT'RY SCENE

PART TWO: THE AMERICAN SCENE

PART THREE: MY SCENE

Part One

The Lit'ry Scene

"The Most Deadly Folly"

January 25, 1982

With a flourish of melodrama, William Styron let it be known last week that his "heart went out" to Norman Mailer over the Jack Henry Abbott case because "I have had an Abbott in my life." Styron's incarcerated protégé escaped from prison and kidnapped and raped a woman, but: "I haven't lost faith in him. I hope to be able to walk through New York City with him some day soon."

Lord have mercy. Why can't Styron just hole up in his affluent Connecticut exurb and write novels, which he does surpassingly well, instead of getting into the newspapers and making a fool of himself? It is almost impossible to conjure up a more ridiculous image of cozy liberal sentimentality than that of Styron and his paroled pen pal strolling together up Fifth Avenue, soon to detour over to Park for luncheon at the Four Seasons. Does Styron's knee jerk in his sleep? Does he really think that he has found a closet Dostoyevsky behind bars? Does he really believe this fellow's art is so overpowering that, if allowed to practice it in the full glow of freedom, he will never again kidnap or rape?

If he really believes all that, then he is as naïve and credulous as Mailer, which is saying something. Mailer, it will be recalled, entered into a correspondence with Abbott, a certifiably rotten apple who was then, as for much of his life, doing time. He was impressed by the quality and force of Abbott's prose, in particular its depiction of the horrors of prison life, and helped him get it published as a book, *In the Belly of the Beast,* which came out last year to great yawps of critical acclaim in all the places you'd expect such yawps. Mailer also endorsed Abbott's application for parole and promised him a job should it be granted. In due time it was, and Abbott was released into the embrace of the New York literati. Six weeks later he killed a man named Richard Adan after a trivial altercation in a restaurant, and he was convicted last week of first-degree manslaughter.

This is what reports have Mailer saying on the subject: The killing of Richard Adan was "absolute tragedy, hideous waste and horror," and "something that the people close to Abbott will have to live with"—which is more than Richard Adan will be able to do. "I'm sorry as hell about the way it turned out," Mailer said, but added, "I'm willing to gamble with certain elements in society to save this man's talent." "Prison," he said, "will destroy this man's talent." And: "Culture is worth a little risk." And: "A major sentence would destroy him. Adan has already been destroyed. At least let Abbott become a writer. . . . It is far too easy to say send him away forever. . . . Society demands you take certain risks. Otherwise, you have a fascistic society."

Cut through all the windy posturing, all the huff and puff ("If you want blood, you can't have my blood. You can have my psychic blood"), and what you have is this: It is worth risking the safety of innocent men and women so that Jack Henry Abbott can be granted the freedom he allegedly needs (bear in mind that *In the Belly of the Beast* was written *in* prison) to develop his "talent." *Ars longa, vita brevis.* Therefore, let the lion prowl the streets, if only the lion will give us Literature.

This is sheer "romanticism," as Edward Albee said, the "assumption . . . that if someone is a gifted writer he deserves . . . treatment above that given to other people." In Albee's penetrating phrase, it is "the most deadly folly." Among those who seem to be seduced by it are Norman Mailer and William Styron—and for a while Jerzy Kosinski, though he got out when the going got hot—men whose reputations bulk large, whether deservedly so or not, in contemporary literature, men presumably of some considerable sophistication and experience.

Don't bet on it. Anyone who has spent a reasonable amount of time in a newsroom is well aware that America's prisons are overflowing with would-be authors. They are forever writing to reporters, editors and columnists, asking for editorial advice and directions to the nearest agent or publisher. Some of their letters seem sincere, others seem manipulative; all have a rather similar ring, in the ways that communiqués from jailhouse lawyers tend to sound the same.

It is impossible for the outsider to tell what's going on—to draw the distinction between a prisoner who has a genuine desire to improve himself and one who merely wants to get out any old way he can. The letters deserve polite replies and, if it can be given, the information they request. But newspaper people have known for decades that these letters can be black holes that will gobble up the unwary. The best strategy is to keep one's distance; the rehabilitation of convicted criminals is for the penal system, not for the city desk or the book-review department.

Nor is it for the Authors Guild—a message that seems not to have gotten through to Mailer and Styron and others of their persuasion. For reasons that seem to have a little to do with genuine sentiment and a lot to do with self-gratification, they have gotten themselves into the penitentiary business—with, in Mailer's case, absolutely disastrous results. That the results in Styron's case will be much better, should his pet criminal gain release, seems unlikely.

These writers look to be playing with the lives of real people much as they might play with the lives of fictitious ones. Jack Henry Abbott wasn't so much Mailer's literary protégé as a feather in his cap: a real live crook—one who writes with his fists!—to be put on exhibit in the salons of radical chic. Jack Henry Abbott was better than a lifetime subscription to *The Nation:* He was walking, talking proof of Mailer's rightmindedness, his concern for the downtrodden, his unwavering commitment to Art. Then Abbott went out and stabbed Richard Adan to death, and Mailer suddenly discovered that he was "obviously a man who is not ready to live quietly in New York society."

Good old Mailer: For everything he has a suave explanation, a nimble rationale. "I didn't read Abbott well enough when he got out because he was such a gentleman," he says, "didn't pay attention to the little warnings he gave me in a quiet little voice." But someone who is listening to the trumpet's blare of his own ego is unlikely to hear any other voices, quiet or otherwise. Still, it's worth a try: The message is that Mailer got involved with Jack Henry Abbott for thrills and didn't bargain for chills. He should stick to his typewriter, where he can order the world any old way he wants. The real one is full of unpleasant surprises, for which in the end someone must be accountable.

Misreading Mark Twain

April 12, 1982

What is perhaps most noteworthy about the bizarre onslaught in Fairfax County, Virginia, against *The Adventures of Huckleberry Finn* is that it arises from a complete misreading of the novel. As interpreted by the members of the Human Relations Committee of (!) Mark Twain Intermediate School, *Huckleberry Finn* bears virtually no resemblance to the novel that Mark Twain actually wrote. One member of that committee, John H. Wallace, describes the novel as follows: "The book is poison. It is anti-American; it works against the melting-pot theory of our country; it works against the idea that all men are created equal; it works against the Fourteenth Amendment to the Constitution and against the Preamble that guarantees all men life, liberty and the pursuit of happiness."

Short of describing *Huckleberry Finn* as crypto-fascist propaganda with socialist-realist, communist-naturalist, secular-humanist influences, it would be difficult to come up with a less perceptive, more wrongheaded reading of the novel. That Wallace's motives are honorable—he believes Twain's depiction of Jim, the runaway slave, is stereotypical and therefore demeaning to blacks, and he wants to shield young readers from it—does not excuse his distortion of the novel's central themes in order to engineer its removal from the classrooms, if not the library, at his school. Further, he makes the crucial mistake of holding a novel written in the late nineteenth century to standards and attitudes that did not become generally accepted until the late twentieth.

While rushing to defend *Huckleberry Finn* against Wallace's attack, I should also hasten to say that I am wholly sympathetic with his reaction to the novel. By the standards that our society observes in 1982, Twain's portrayal of Jim and his incessant use of the word "nigger" *are* offensive. That "nigger" was commonly and casually employed in 1884, when the novel was published, and that Jim's dialect and behavior are probably faithful to the time and place, do not make either the language or the stereotype any easier to swallow for the late twentieth-century reader, whatever his or her color.

But however understandable and legitimate Wallace's objections may be, his reading of the novel is astonishingly superficial—and, for a professional educator, downright irresponsible. Looking at *Huckleberry Finn* as he does, all that Wallace seems to see is the recurrence of "nigger" and the depiction of Jim as a precursor of Stepin Fetchit. No doubt he would dismiss, and despise, this paragraph as "racist":

"I went to sleep, and Jim didn't call me when it was my turn. He often done that. When I waked up just at daybreak he was sitting there with his head down betwixt his knees, moaning and mourning to himself. I didn't take notice nor let on. I knowed what it was about. He was thinking about his wife and his children, away up yonder, and he was low and homesick; because he hadn't ever been away from home before in his life; and I do believe he cared just as much for his people as white folks does for their'n. It don't seem natural, but I reckon it's so. He was often moaning and mourning that way nights, when he judged I was asleep, and saying, 'Po' little 'Lizabeth! po' little Johnny! it's mighty hard; I spec' I ain't ever gwyne to see you no mo', no mo'!' He was a mighty good nigger, Jim was."

The point of this passage is not that Jim is a "nigger" who talks like a stereotype, but that he is a human being with feelings and urges as deep and complex as those of the white boy who observes him—if not, in fact, considerably deeper and more complex. Another point is that this boy, raised by a racist father in a racist society, comes to understand and value Jim's humanity through prolonged, intimate association with him. Yet another point is that Twain, a native Southerner, wrote *Huckleberry Finn* at a time when the slightest suggestion of sympathy for blacks was regarded as unseemly both north and south of the Mason–Dixon Line; yet as his biographer, Justin Kaplan, has observed, Twain had "explicit sympathy for the Negro" and a "level vision of the brutalities of a slaveholding society," and he had the courage to express these views when all but the smallest minority were in violent disagreement with them.

It is, when you pause to reflect upon it, preposterous—not to mention ludicrous, outrageous and absurd—that in what represents itself as an enlightened age we should have to defend Mark Twain, of all people, and his great novel, of all books, against an attack so petty and pusillanimous as this one. What is perhaps even more preposterous is that this attack is being made, its leaders allege, in defense of precisely the same virtues that Twain celebrated in *Huckleberry Finn:* freedom, humanity, decency, equality, humility, simple kindness.

That being the case, I can only assume that Wallace and his Human Relations Committee have undertaken this wholly gratuitous enterprise because they do not have the foggiest idea what *Huckleberry Finn* is about. If that is so, what in heaven's name are they doing presiding over the education of the young? Would they ban *Moby-Dick* as vivisectionist, or *The Great Gatsby* as anti-Semitic? If these men and women cannot identify the most basic themes of a work of fiction that for nearly a century has been explicated to a fare-thee-well by critics, scholars and ordinary students, then perhaps they should find another line of work.

Or else, since they are educators, they could take a stab at educating. Instead of retreating behind the curtain of censorship, they could try to tell their students what America was like in 1884 and what Mark Twain was saying, in *Huckleberry Finn,* about that society. They could point out to their students, if indeed they understood it themselves, that *Huckleberry Finn* is, beneath its veneer of satire and folk humor, a dark and tormented meditation upon the conflict between the individual's yearning for freedom and friendship on the one hand and the restrictions and prejudices imposed by society on the other. They could point out that "nigger," a word that we now properly regard as an obscenity, was then in general use among the genteel as well as the vulgar.

They could point out, were they so inclined, that if anything it is a measure of how far we have progressed that we are uncomfortable with things in *Huckleberry Finn* that were accepted as normal when it was published and long thereafter. They could point out that the human capacity for moral and social growth is marvelous, but that such growth cannot diminish the greatness of a work of art. Do we spurn *Othello* because of the Moor or *The Merchant of Venice* because of Shylock? Of course not. We look instead to the works of art, and to the extraordinary human being who made them. We do not dismiss them as bigoted because their author was not so fortunate as to live in an age that regards itself as holding a monopoly on righteousness, an age that regards the longstanding popularity of *The Jeffersons* as evidence of its commitment to racial tolerance.

Well. *Huckleberry Finn* has had its other critics. In the spring of 1885, Louisa May Alcott complained ("If Mr. Clemons cannot think of something better to tell our pure-minded lads and lasses, he had best stop writing for them"), and the novel was banned by the Library Committee of Concord, Massachusetts. It survived that blow, and it will survive this one. In fact, it should not come as a bit of a surprise if, as a result of the publicity afforded it by John H. Wallace and the other guardians of "human relations," the novel enjoys a hearty revival in Fairfax County and environs. That would be good news, and a twist that its author would have enjoyed.

"Rabbit" Isn't Rich

April 26, 1982

Tomorrow evening in New York, John Updike will receive the 1982 American Book Award in Fiction for his novel *Rabbit Is Rich*—the third major literary prize to be lavished upon this latest account of the adventures, libidinous and otherwise, of Harry "Rabbit" Angstrom. That so much glory should have descended upon this novel is one of the great mysteries of the age; surely it is proof positive, as if further proof were needed, that we do not live in a meritocracy.

For this exercise in self-indulgence and self-importance, Updike has already received the fiction awards bestowed by the National Book Critics Circle and the Pulitzer Prizes. Only the PEN/Faulkner Award, which in its brief existence has made a concentrated effort to be "different," has eluded Updike; it went to a deserving writer, David Bradley, for an interesting and intelligent but perhaps undeserving novel, *The Chaneysville Incident*.

Still, three out of four isn't bad; not even the redoubtable Eddie Murray of the Baltimore Orioles is batting .750 this spring. Had all of this praise gone to one of Updike's earlier books—*Rabbit, Run*, or *Bech: A Book*, or even *Couples*—it would have been well earned. But in fact Updike's earlier and vastly better books went, for whatever reason, almost entirely unnoticed by the people who make it their business to hand out honors; only a Rosenthal Award, granted to Updike in 1960 for *The Poorhouse Fair* by the National Institute of Arts and Letters, decorated his escutcheon until this sudden thunderclap of applause. Now, for a thoroughly bad novel, he has acquired a lifetime's worth of plaques, scrolls and checks.

This of course is not without precedent. It has always been something of a rarity for an American novelist to receive a major award for his best work. Faulkner got no Pulitzer in 1937 for *Absalom! Absalom!* (it went that year, irony of ironies, to *Gone With the Wind*), but received one almost two decades later for the gassily unreadable *A Fable*. Ditto for Hemingway, who was passed over in 1927 for *The Sun Also Rises* but, a quarter century later, was granted one for *The Old Man and the Sea*, a work of exquisite fatuousness. Institutions that hand out awards tend to be conservative and to climb aboard literary bandwagons only after their forward progress has been halted.

In Updike's case it is to be hoped that it is not so; he has just this year turned fifty, which is far too early an age for a writer to run out of gas—even if, in *Rabbit Is Rich*, he has written a novel about an America running out of gas. But there can be little question that *Rabbit Is Rich* is on almost every count an inferior piece of work. Whether it is actually Updike's worst book is open to question, since when he is bad (*A Month of Sundays*, *Marry Me*, *Rabbit Redux*), he is awful; what is not open to argument, at least so far as I see it, is that the novel puts on display all of Updike's worst characteristics.

Like its predecessor *Rabbit Redux*, *Rabbit Is Rich* exists less for the creation of characters and social textures—at which Updike can be superbly skilled—than for the elaboration of Updike's political and social viewpoints. He is under the mistaken impression that he has interesting things to say about these matters, and he says them in a loud, insistent voice. *Rabbit Is Rich* is a novel of pushy, intrusive topicality, serving up its author's opinions on everything from Jimmy Carter's jogging to the gas lines to Skylab; it's fiction as op-edit page, and it doesn't work as either. To wit:

". . . On the news, there is rioting in Levittown over gasoline, people are throwing beer bottles full of gasoline; they explode, it looks like old films of Vietnam or Budapest but it is Levittown right down the road, north of Philadelphia. A striking trucker is shown holding up a sign saying TO HELL WITH SHELL. And Three-Mile Island leaking radioactive neutrons just down the road in the other direction. The weather for tomorrow looks good, as a massive high continues to dominate from the Rocky Mountain region eastward all the way to Maine. Time for bed."

Which is where all good Updike characters go when, as it so often does, the spirit moves them. In *Rabbit Is Rich*, Updike is trying to write about the contrast between middle-aged sexual desire and middle-aged sexual performance, but he smothers a legitimate subject and some legitimate ideas about it under a great weight of gratuitous (and, in my stuffy view, tasteless) sexual detail. He seems to have the idea that it is bold and meaningful to dwell, in the most monotonous imaginable length and particularity, upon the shape, color and odor of various organs, not to mention the various tricks they can perform when introduced to each other. He believes himself, so far as I can tell, to treat these subjects with wit, sympathy and candor; it does not seem to have occurred to him that he is merely vulgar.

Indeed, *Rabbit Is Rich* reeks of vulgarity. Updike fancies himself the chronicler of the common man, and he fills page after page with the most clinical evidence of that poor fellow's gaucherie. So far as I can determine, he also believes that he portrays the common man with sympathy and understanding. Yet what come through most vividly in *Rabbit Is Rich* are Updike's contempt and condescension. Gazing down from his aerie north of Boston, he sees nothing except tackiness:

"The chair Peggy sits in is squared-off ponderous modern with a pale fabric thick as plywood; it matches another chair and a long sofa set around that kind of table with no overhang to the top they call a Parsons table, which is put together in alternating blocks of light and dark wood, with a curly knotty grain such as they make golf club heads of. The entire deep space of the room, which Webb added on when he and Cindy acquired this house in the pace-setting development of Brewer Heights, gently brims with appointments chosen all to harmonize. Its tawny wallpaper has vertical threads of texture in it like the vertical folds of the slightly darker pull drapes, and reproductions of Wyeth watercolors lit by spots on track lighting overhead echo with scratchy strokes the same tints, and the same lighting reveals little sparkles, like mica on a beach, in the overlapping arcs of the rough-plastered ceiling . . ."

If *that* doesn't make you feel superior, nothing will. Beneath its façade of sympathy for the poor ordinary man trying to find meaning in his life, *Rabbit Is Rich* is one extended sneer at American society as exemplified by that very same ordinary man. Which gets us to one possible explanation for the awards with which it is now festooned: it expresses, in a culturally acceptable fashion, the political and social prejudices of the literati. It allows the reader, just as it allows the author, to pretend to be egalitarian while simultaneously he turns up his nose at democratic man. The novel is a masquerade in which the reader is invited to participate.

At the same time, it offers the upper-middle-class reader the chance to go slumming, a diversion in which the intellectually as well as the financially privileged take unflagging pleasure. What could be more gratifying than to wallow around in—while carefully keeping one's distance from—a world of tacky people who live in tacky houses filled with tacky furniture, who watch tacky television shows and eat tacky food while thinking tacky thoughts? Further, it's all so jammed with details—brand names and song titles and headlines—that you're just as sure as sure can be that Updike has penetrated to the very heart of American darkness. It seems not to have occurred to anyone that he has penetrated to nothing more substantial than the heart of his own straw man.

But all of this is after the fact. The awards have been made, and *Rabbit Is Rich* has been handed over to the ages. The guess here is that they will take one look at it and bar the door. *Rabbit*

Is Rich is a creature of its moment and, more to the point, of a tiny hothouse culture within that moment. When the moment passes, as soon enough it will, *Rabbit Is Rich* will pass right along with it. A quarter century from now, if not sooner, it will be gone and quite forgotten.

Poor Little Rich Man

March 14, 1983

The mind of John le Carré, as revealed in his fine novels, is a Byzantine and mysterious place, filled with bottomless pools of ambiguity and dark tunnels that wind from here to uncertainty. But on one question it is startlingly direct: the moral superiority of suffering and deprivation.

This is a principal theme of le Carré's new novel, *The Little Drummer Girl*, in which a pampered young woman of the privileged West is forced to confront the despair of the Middle East, in one scene personified by a leader of Palestinian forces: ". . . he spoke from pains she had not experienced, from a viewpoint she had yet to learn. He was not old, but he had a wisdom that had been acquired too early." Or as le Carré put it more directly in a recent interview with *Newsweek:* "I've always had a frightful contempt for the self-indulgent dilemmas of affluent Western man, compared to the experiences of real hell, of people who spent twenty years in jail for almost immaterial reasons."

This is, at first inspection, unexceptionable. Is le Carré talking about the tendency of certain affluent Westerners to dash off to Dr. Feelgood at the merest quiver or quaver of their fragile psyches? If he is, then of course he is right. Is he talking about the tendency of these same Westerners to indulge themselves in great wallows of self-pity because the revenue service wants to have a chat with them or the assessment on the house has gone up or a lover has found a better offer? If he is, then, again, of course he is right.

But it is not at all clear that this is in fact what he has in mind. Rather, there is a good deal of evidence that le Carré has fallen for one of the persistent pieties of Western sentimentalism: that one of the chief obligations of privilege is guilt. It is a variation, albeit a subtle one, on the impulse that led parents of an earlier generation to bear in mind the starving children of India as they contemplated their uneaten spinach; the underlying assumption is that there is a direct relationship between the prosperity of the West and the impoverishment of the rest of the world, and that it is therefore the responsibility of the West to do penance.

There *is* a direct relationship in the crucial sense that a substantial measure of the comforts enjoyed by the prosperous come at the expense of the impoverished, i.e., through the exploitation of their natural and human resources. But this, though most emphatically deplorable and a wholly valid reason for anti-Western sentiment, is not what le Carré and others of like persuasion are talking about. Their argument, stripped of whatever adornments may accompany it, is that Western affluence is morally bankrupt, that the cares of the fortunate are inherently trivial, that the only "real" world—the only world worth caring about—is the one where injustice and the whimsical twists of malign fate are daily givens, where life is *hard.*

The difficulty in disagreeing with this argument is that it's just about impossible to avoid sounding smug, complacent and arrogant when stating one's disagreement. Yet it is not merely supercilious to ask precisely what the Westerner of conscience reasonably can be expected to do in order to rectify the situation, in order to put matters into equitable balance. Wear a hair shirt? Wrap CARE packages? Take forty lashes a day? Enter a nunnery? Tithe? Go to jail? Fast? Would the Westerner who inflicted any of these punishments on himself in any way alter the distance between the prosperous and the impoverished? Certainly not. He would only massage, and display for all to see, his guilt and his moral superiority.

This is arrogance of a different kind, one not notably more

attractive than that of the "affluent Western man" who self-indulgently ships his ego out for psychiatric repairs. In the specific case of le Carré, there's also what looks for all the world like a strong element of hypocrisy. It is not easy to swallow a lecture on "what passed for pain in Western middle-class society" (as le Carré phrases it in the novel) from one whose well-deserved successes have made him, according to *Newsweek*, "a rich man" whose family "divides its time between a rambling house in London and an imposing stone house in rural Cornwall, on the southwesternmost tip of the English coast, with a sweeping view of the sea"—and who, although he "guards his privacy fiercely," recently has allowed it to be violated by correspondents of *Newsweek* and other publications for the purpose of promoting his new book and thus assuring himself and his publishers still further wealth.

Is it unfair to dwell on this? Hardly. Sermonizing about the decadence of affluent society has a hollow ring indeed when the preacher is one who has supped so lavishly at that society's table. Perhaps le Carré would argue that by writing so eloquently as he does in *The Little Drummer Girl* about the agonies of the Middle East, he has paid his dues to the world's unfortunate, and perhaps he has. But that does not entitle him to moral posturings of the sort in which he engages when he natters on about the banality of "Western middle-class society."

Le Carré to the contrary, suffering and deprivation are not virtues that separate the morally correct from the morally bankrupt. Pain does not elevate; it is merely painful. And in any event the impoverished of the world do not have a monopoly on pain, though that which they suffer certainly is far worse than the woes usually visited upon the more privileged. Pain varies according to the circumstances one has been dealt; no doubt it is true that the pain of a struggle for mere survival is deeper—"better," if you will—than the pain of trying to determine if one's life has any meaning or pertinence, but it remains that neither is any fun for the person undergoing it.

Yes: Life is hell for the Palestinian refugees and for millions of others to whom fate has been unspeakably cruel. But it is not axiomatic that because they suffer, those in happier situations are contemptible—and it is a pity that a writer of sensibilities so acute as le Carré's should succumb to so fatuous a line of reasoning.

Books That "Comfort"

April 18, 1983

Sympathy and gratitude were, no doubt, the responses of many readers to a letter to the editor published last week in the *Washington Post* under the headline THAT'S A CLASSIC? With considerable eloquence and passion, its author addressed a question that has troubled mothers and fathers for as long as children have been force-fed the alleged masterpieces of world literature: Why does my child have to read this book?

The letter to the editor was occasioned by its author's discovery that her sixteen-year-old daughter was being required to read John Steinbeck's *The Grapes of Wrath* in a Northern Virginia high school. Recalling that she had read the same novel at the same age, and that she had "hated it," the mother took the trouble to read it once again. "Now I remember why I hated it so," she wrote, "and I know my daughter well enough to know that she will hate it as much, if not more, than I did." She added: "And so it continues, generation after generation. Because they carry the label of 'classics,' sordid, dreary, depressing books continue to be forced upon eager, questing young minds. Like me, my daughter is an insatiable reader. I pray that also, like me, books will be her doorway to new worlds, exciting personalities, refreshing, comforting ideas her whole life long."

She wondered why it is that "when there is so much literature that can stimulate, encourage, gladden, improve a life," a book such as *The Grapes of Wrath* is required high-school reading, and concluded: "I don't know how many times I have heard a young person say, 'I hate that book, it is so depressing, and I have to read it to get a grade!' What a sad statement about our teaching methods. No wonder so many young people never learn the joys of reading."

This letter raises several interesting points. The first and most trivial is the puzzling intelligence that *The Grapes of Wrath* is represented in a high-school English course as a "classic" of literature. It is indeed a work of considerable power, but that derives from the ardor of its political and social commentary rather than from any particular literary qualities. Like Upton Sinclair's *The Jungle,* it is a polemic in the guise of a novel, and Steinbeck's purposes in writing it were as much political as literary: He wanted to call the nation's attention to the plight of the Dust Bowl refugees, and he succeeded. But ever since its publication readers have confused the high-mindedness of Steinbeck's sentiments with literary accomplishment and have accorded the novel a reverent respect that, in purely literary terms, it simply does not deserve.

But whatever the shortcomings of its prose and structure, *The Grapes of Wrath* cannot be dismissed as "sordid, dreary, depressing" and "destructive." How can this novel be described, as it is in this letter, as a "classic example of archaic thinking that, as happens throughout history, will be proven not necessarily so, and changed to the benefit of many"? Is *The Grapes of Wrath* a "sordid" book because it depicts ours as a society whose riches are unjustly distributed? Is it a "dreary" book because it portrays the lives of the Okies as desperate and hopeless? Is it a "depressing" book because it shows a side of American life that those of us more comfortably situated would prefer to tell ourselves does not exist? Is it a "destructive" book because it arouses guilt and discomfort in some readers?

It is difficult to interpret this letter otherwise, because it's a letter that speaks, forcefully and articulately, for a point of view that has always had wide currency—a view that literature should be uplifting and affirmative, that it should deliver the "good news" about the human condition and thus elevate the minds of its readers, that it should offer what our correspondent describes as "comforting ideas." Well, if that be literature, then we had best get about cleaning off the shelves, and when we are finished there will be precious little save *Pollyanna* and *Rebecca of Sunnybrook Farm* and Parson Weems's life of George Washington.

There'll be no more Shakespeare: *King Lear* is sordid, *Hamlet* is dreary, *Macbeth* is depressing, *Julius Caesar* is destructive. Good-bye, Dickens: *Bleak House* is, well, bleak, and *Great Expectations* depicts quite the wrong side of English society. You can forget Faulkner: All those sordid Southerners doing sordid things to each other, not to mention Popeye and that appalling corncob. Go back to Poland, Conrad: *Victory* has no comforting ideas and *Heart of Darkness* gets more depressing with every page. So much for the ancient Greeks—they're much too *tragic*—and the nineteenth-century Russians, with all their crimes and punishments.

The last thing we want is to expose our children to books (or paintings, or musical compositions, or movies) that suggest there's anything to life except sunshine and Santa Claus. If we shield them from the alarms and discords of human existence, then presumably there will be no alarms and discords in their lives. With their heads snuggled comfortably in the sand, they'll live happily ever after—blissfully oblivious to the cold reality that this world can be, even for a middle-class American, hard and unjust and bitterly unrewarding.

Those, of course, are among the many realities that help nurture worthwhile and important books, whether they be tough polemical novels such as *The Jungle* or *The Grapes of Wrath* or masterpieces of literature such as *King Lear* or *Light in August.* The "joys of reading" these books offer are not, to be sure, the same as the joys that come with being told God's in his heaven and all's right with the world; but might it not be suggested, however tentatively, that they are deeper and more substantial joys?

Literature is like life: It is hard. One of the chief reasons we send our children to school is so that they will learn to recognize hard things for what they are and to develop ways of coping with them. A child raised on nothing except good news and "comforting ideas" will become an adult almost certainly incapable of meeting life on its own tough terms. A child who has been taught to deal equably with ideas and facts he doesn't much like, on the other hand, will be admirably equipped for the struggle ahead—and, in the bargain, will be an interesting person.

New Life for the Novel

December 12, 1983

In an otherwise chipper acceptance address for his Nobel Prize in Literature, the British novelist William Golding spoke gloomily last week about the future of the medium in which he labors. The novel, he said, threatens to become "a stopgap for when there are no Westerns on the television" and as such may have only a brief life remaining. If it cannot find new vitality and a steady audience, he said, "let the novel go; we have enough complications in life, in art, in literature without cluttering ourselves with Byzantine sterilities."

The point is sound: Institutions that struggle to stay alive long after they have lost pertinence and interest are anachronisms; efforts to pump them full of air are what give preservationism a bad name. So if the novel is dying, if it no longer has anything arresting to say and no audience wants to listen to its empty messages, then by all means let it go, the sooner the better. Bring on the videocassette recorders and the home-entertainment centers, and to all a good night.

Yet almost all available evidence suggests that this would be a premature burial. Like anything else that depends for its existence on the fragile workings of the creative impulse, the novel goes through unpredictable phases. A couple of decades ago it was widely considered not merely to be dying but to be dead, the victim of that allegedly superior form, the "nonfiction novel." What happened, though—as recently demonstrated by Thomas Keneally's *Schindler's List*—is exactly the opposite, as the novel merely absorbed the "nonfiction novel." But now, if

William Golding and others are to be believed, it is television that lurks in the dark alley, ready to pounce on the poor unsuspecting novel.

Don't put your money on it. This Lazarus has risen too many times in the past. If mass-circulation magazines couldn't do it in, or motion pictures, or radio, or drive-in theaters, who is to say that the sitcoms and cop shows of television will be its executioners? *Collier's*, *The Jazz Singer*, *Amos 'n' Andy*, the Starlite Drive-In, *Your Show of Shows*—these and innumerable others like them are gone and largely forgotten, but the novel struggles on.

To be sure, a case can be made that it struggles fitfully. In England much interesting fiction has been written in recent years, but virtually all of it has been comfy and undemanding; only Graham Greene among living British writers consistently takes on great themes and assumes large risks, and in any event at this point in his career is less a British writer than an international one. As for the United States, there are indeed writers who attempt to address themselves to pressing and difficult questions, but more and more American fiction is dominated by the self-absorption of the creative-writing schools and the Manhattanite provincialism of the publishing industry; neither characteristic bodes well for the novel in this country, since each is hostile to the interests and experiences of readers—probably we should call them ex-readers—outside its own sphere.

But in the part of the world that is variously and inadequately described as "underdeveloped" or "developing" or "third," the novel these days is proving itself a medium of extraordinary force and immediacy. The 1983 Nobel to Golding is of far less significance than the 1982 prize to Gabriel García Márquez, the Colombian novelist whose work and personal example have inspired countless writers in other countries. These writers have found that the novel is an ideal form in which to confront contemporary realities that they regard as fantastic, bewildering, outrageous and hilarious. A clear case in point is Salman Rushdie's fine new novel, *Shame*, in which he rejects the "realistic novel" as an impossibility when writing about Pakistan and offers this wry commentary:

"By now, if I had been writing a [realistic] book of this nature, it would have done me no good to protest that I was writing universally, not only about Pakistan. The book would have been banned, dumped in the rubbish bin, burned. All that effort for nothing! Rubbish can break a writer's heart.

"Fortunately, however, I am only telling a sort of modern fairy tale, so that's all right; nobody need get upset, or take anything I say too seriously. No drastic action need be taken, either.

"What a relief!"

The tone is mocking but the observation is penetrating. The novel, within which the writer is free to create any world that arises in his imagination, offers a way out in societies where the repression of journalism and social commentary is often chilling. Writers such as Rushdie, García Márquez and J. M. Coetzee of South Africa—all concerned in their particular ways with the human longing for freedom in an oppressive world—can rise in the novel from the specific to the universal; the novel permits them to cast aside immediate and transitory political matters, to get to the deeper and more lasting themes that the histories of their countries suggest.

The novel also offers them a way to confront contemporary realities that, viewed through the clinical eye of the television camera or the newspaper report, almost defy rational description. How can one adequately describe the reality of much of Central America, where human life no longer has any value? Or the reality of the subcontinent, where people by the uncounted thousands starve in the streets? Or the reality of much of Africa, where interracial hostilities determine the routine course of daily existence?

The novelists have found one way: It is what Rushdie calls the "modern fairy tale." The operative assumption behind it is that since these realities already transcend our capacity to comprehend them, then perhaps we can see them more clearly by exaggerating them into entirely new dimensions—into phantasmagorical worlds of magic, madness and exuberance that offer, however improbably, a mirror image of our own. This is what García Márquez in *One Hundred Years of Solitude* and Rushdie in *Midnight's Children* have done on the panoramic scale; it is also what Coetzee has done, on the fabulist's miniature scale, in *Waiting for the Barbarians.*

Certainly it is possible that in the West the novel is, if not dying, in a state of exhaustion; how many more tales about Oxford dons and New York career women is an intelligent readership willing to accommodate? But out there in the "other" world, the novel may well be entering a period of greatness not seen since the high Victorian era. Can it be that its most rewarding diet is that of upheaval and outrage?

Mary McCarthy's Dreamland

January 2, 1984

Here we are a mere two days into the new year and the silly season has already started. It was launched yesterday morning, before the aspirin and/or the bloody Marys had enough time to make the day ahead seem tolerable, by the redoubtable Mary McCarthy, the well-known chronicler of upper-crust manners and dabbler in matters political. Writing in *The New York Times Book Review,* McCarthy addressed herself to the political novel and opined: "Americans, I think, tend to get their political education through fiction—occasionally through poetry, though this is becoming rarer."

Right. And wishes are horses so beggars shall ride, and there's gold at the end of the rainbow, and the check is in the mail. Has McCarthy recently moved to Fool's Paradise? The mere notion that fiction seriously influences the political opinions of Americans—that, as she put it elsewhere, "fictions do sway us to the right or left, and Americans, I suspect, more than most"—is pure twaddle, though, to be sure, twaddle of the sort with which certain literati like to delude themselves.

By way of proving the point, not to mention elevating the personal into the universal, McCarthy cited her own journey along the road to her literary Damascus. She was "in my senior year at Vassar in Miss Peeble's course in Contemporary Fiction" (!) when she came smack up against *The 42nd Parallel,* the first volume in John Dos Passos's trilogy *U.S.A.* You could have knocked her over with a quill: "Though I did not yet realize it, it was the Book of Lancelot for me: '*Quel giorno più non vi leggemmo avante'* (That day we read in it no farther), or, putting it in Manzonian terms, *'La Sventurata rispose'*—I responded."

Indeed she did. This self-described "arch-conservative" and "royalist" suddenly "fell madly in love" with a book that paid powerful tribute to the exploited masses and delivered equally powerful attacks on their privileged exploiters. She was fascinated by the novel's mixture of fictional and historical characters: "The one I most took to was Mac, who became a Wobbly or at any rate a socialist and was killed young. Best of all, I loved Debs, among the biographies, and disliked J. P. Morgan most." So off she soared, on gossamer wings, into the cozy world of thirties leftism: "One thing leading to another, soon after graduation, I was writing little book reviews for the *New Republic,* then for the *Nation,* and I never looked back. Like a Japanese paper flower dropped into a glass of water, it all unfolded, magically, from Dos Passos. . . ."

That's a fact. A schoolgirl crush on Eugene V. Debs and Big Bill Haywood, as immortalized by Dos Passos, blossomed into a celebrated literary/political career that made McCarthy a household name, at least in certain households—those with subscriptions to all the right magazines, memberships in the Vassar Alumni Association and summer places in Provincetown. She proved that if you blend a schoolgirl crush with a considerable gift for invective, you get something very close to dynamite, and she exploded all over the pages of *The Nation* and other journals similarly inclined. She also proved that, yes, it really is possible to have your cake and eat it too—she acquired over the years a pleasing identification with resoundingly egalitarian causes, while at the same time she attained the best-seller lists with novels about the professoriat (*The Groves of Academe*) and prosperous matrons (*The Group*).

She did not prove, though, that Americans "tend to get their political education through fiction," nor did she persuasively argue that point in yesterday's rambling, precious examination of novels having real or imagined political overtones. The problem lies not in the specific books she cites as having political themes and thus political consequences, but in the underlying assumption of her essay. "To make the point," she wrote, "there is no need to seek to prove (as some academic recently did) that *Moby-Dick* is an allegory of capitalism. What is interesting is that so many of the novels I have been naming have been high on the best-seller lists. The political novel in this country is certainly no fringe phenomenon."

These words appeared in the same newspaper that only two days earlier had quoted a prominent executive of the paperback publishing industry as saying: "Our job, in a business that's described as mass market, is to keep five million people, maybe ten million, out of two hundred and twenty million people, responsive to our product. We're a very easy habit to give up. Reading is not like watching television, it's something you have to work at. And our job as publishers is to survive." The point should need no elaboration: In a country where the most wildly optimistic of publishers sees the "mass" market for paperback books as being 4.5 percent of the population, it is preposterous to suggest—not to mention insist—that political fiction has any serious influence on the political views of the electorate.

McCarthy, need it be said, was not talking about the kind of fiction that most of this 4.5 percent is likely to read. She was talking about literary works, of a pronouncedly leftist bias, that appeal to a literary readership—one that might be estimated, by a litterateur given to exaggerated self-delusion, at perhaps two million souls, or less than 1 percent of the population. It is, to be sure, 1 percent that is "elite" and "visible" and "influential" far out of proportion to its numbers, but it is still, when you get right down to it, 1 percent.

If American political opinion really was influenced by American political fiction, we most certainly would be living in a very different nation from the one we now inhabit. With the notable exceptions of books by James Gould Cozzens, Dos Passos in his later years, and Allen Drury (who, interestingly, goes unmentioned in McCarthy's chronicle), American political novels have come from the left of center. They have tended to be sympathetic to the masses (*The Grapes of Wrath*), opposed to warfare (*Catch-22*), and hostile to professional politicians (*All the King's Men*). Anyone who believes that American government today reflects any of these views needs to have his eyes examined and his equilibrium corrected.

But then McCarthy never really was talking about the real world Out There. She was talking about the little world of the literati, in which if you close your eyes, take a deep breath and make a wish you can actually convince yourself that E. L. Doctorow and Joseph Heller are political figures of stature and influence. From there it is just a short distance—why, no more than a baby step—to persuading yourself that Doctorow and Heller, not to mention Arthur Miller and Philip Roth and all the other guardians of the literary conscience, are the real shapers of American political thought. And from there, who knows where you can go? So long as you keep your eyes closed, you can go anywhere at all.

The Lit'ry Life: I

February 27, 1984

Today may be the last Monday in February, but in the garrets and libraries where writers dwell it might as well be spring. This is because—for reasons long since lost in the haze of memory—the publishing industry has made it a practice to decree as "spring" the period that begins in February and ends as late as July. Thus it is that for writers around the country, the awful moment of truth is now about to descend: Their books, nurtured in the isolation of their dens and fens, are about to see the light of day.

"Waiting for publication day" is what the process is called, and if Satan in his diabolical cruelty has invented a fouler torture for middle-class man, word of it has not reached these quarters. The process of publication takes, from delivery of a manuscript until production of a finished book, about nine months, and the obvious comparison is indeed apt: Having a book is every bit as difficult as having a baby, except that frequently the end results are considerably less pleasant. Babies usually grow up to be nice people with houses and jobs and bank accounts; books usually grow up to be remainders.

Except for the very fortunate—and very few—authors whose books actually fulfill all the expectations invested in them, the publication of a book is one of life's most disenchanting, albeit instructive, experiences. It begins with an intoxicating high and ends, more often than not, with a demoralizing low; the gates to immortality that at first seem to beckon turn out, more often than not, to be the gates to perdition. Why on earth do people pass through them?

The answer is simple: because every writer believes that he will be the exception to the rule. Is there a stronger or deeper strain in human nature than the one that says, It can't happen to me? Besides, when the process starts everything looks so rosy that it is quite impossible to see the dark at the end of the tunnel. For the writer just delivering his manuscript to his publisher, there seems nowhere to go but up; yet history tells him, though of course he is not listening, that there is nowhere to go except down, down, down.

In the beginning there is the incredible rush that comes from completing a manuscript. Though there is a certain sadness attendant to typing "The End" and pulling that last page out of the typewriter—it's the literary equivalent of postpartum depression—it doesn't last for long. The labor that has taken hold of your life for so many months, or so many years, has at last been concluded. The impossible has been achieved. You've done it! Your book is wonderful, and so are you!

Which is exactly what everyone at your publishing house tells you, even as their grasping hands take your manuscript into custody and remove it forever from your own control. "We're proud to publish you," they tell you. Stroke, stroke, stroke. "We expect major reviews." Stroke, stroke, stroke. "Copies go out to the book clubs this week." Stroke, stroke, stroke. "You'll get a half page in the spring catalog." Stroke, stroke, stroke. "Just wait until you see the stunning jacket." Stroke, stroke, stroke.

Who are you to know what's going on here? All of these smart, stylish people are lathering you from head to toe, and it feels *great.* They take you out to lunch, maybe even to the Four Seasons, and they smile indulgently as you drink their tax-deductible gin. "Have another, and by all means order the venison *paillard.*" With the wine you toast Johann Gutenberg, Maxwell Perkins and B. Dalton. "Let's go back to the office and talk about the next contract." Righto!

You fly home under your own power, but when you land a funny thing happens. *Nothing* happens. The phone does *not* ring every fifteen minutes. The mail does *not* bring a check every day, or an invitation to the White House, or rhapsodic blurbs from Arthur M. Schlesinger, Jr., Robert Penn Warren or James Dickey. Finally, you can't stand the silence any longer. You pick up the phone and call your editor. And what does the secretary tell you? Your editor is busy with—can you believe this?—*other authors!*

Then the galley proofs arrive. Your moment of pride, right? Your immortal words in type, right? Grinning madly you take out your red pen and start proofreading. Hey! What's going on here? What happened to all your commas? Why have all your semicolons been turned into dashes? What idiot has been playing around with this thing, anyway?

It takes you two full days to fix the damned galleys, and when your publisher gets them back he tries to hit you with correction charges; thank heavens for your agent, who quickly calls a halt to that. But a message is beginning to seep through: This is not quite as much fun as you'd thought it was going to be. Contrary to all your most ardent expectations, the world does not seem to be waiting breathlessly to read your words—a suspicion that deepens when your editor tells you that the first printing, which in your mind you'd set at 35,000, will be a cool 7,500.

Then come the early reviews. *Publishers Weekly:* "Promising but flawed." It's only 10:30 A.M., but you pour yourself a martini. *Library Journal:* "Intelligent but presumptuous." You take a long walk, pausing from time to time to lean against a tree and sob. *Kirkus Reviews:* "Well written but poorly structured." You've had five clean years, but you sprint to the corner store and buy a pack of cigarettes. Two packs. They'll taste good with three martinis. Make that four.

Is this the end? Not on your life. This is the *beginning.* The worst is yet to come. The jacket, for instance: its garish depiction of a comely woman on a wind-swept hill would go nicely on a gothic romance, but it hardly suits your lit'ry masterpiece. Then the publicity department calls. "Uh, sorry about that, but we're dropping the West Coast from your tour. And Chicago. And Boston. And Cleveland. Well, actually, what we have for you is a nice radio interview here in New York. A couple of student newspapers have expressed interest. The publication party? We thought we'd have a nice wine and cheese here in the office, then dinner at Sizzler."

And then—sorry about that, but this is reality—the reviewers check in. "Promising but flawed": Suddenly it's become the story of your life. The book seems to have been assigned for review to everyone who has a silent vendetta against you. "Promising but flawed": Were crueler words ever written? Well, yes, as a matter of fact they were. By the sales department: total sales, 3,471. Remainder tables, here you come.

But for all of that, take heart. Here, from one who has been through it all and lived to tell the tale, is the good news: You'll get over it. It may take years and a couple of slander suits, but you'll get over it. Someday the tears will dry and the alcohol will evaporate, and on that day you'll suck in your gut, take a deep breath and . . . what will you do? You'll go back to your typewriter, you ninny.

The New Orthodoxy

July 9, 1984

It is the contention of Benjamin DeMott, writing in *The New York Times Book Review,* that the 1960s were a "killer decade" for American fiction. DeMott, who is an English professor at Amherst College, surveys the work of writers "nearing or entering into their forties" and concludes, gloomily, that "the most interesting of these writers sometimes seem actually to be secret collaborators bent on telling one and only one story, the changeless theme of which is human unresponsiveness." The blame for this he places in familiar quarters:

"We are speaking of writers-to-be who grew up in an age when their homeland was known as a brutal, barbarous bully raging to burn the entire helpless population of Southeast Asia, an age when dawning awareness of the homeland as a sly, self-deceiving oppressor was followed almost instantly by assassinations, riots and separatist movements that made it impossible to translate the awareness into practical correctives, an age when middle-class youth was instructed by its elders to hide out from the draft on university campuses while working-class children were blown apart *pro patria.* . . . [These writers] tell us repeatedly that they are children of their time."

What we have here is an argument that gets about halfway, perhaps not quite that far, to the plausible. DeMott is right in characterizing the 1960s as an unhappy and unhealthy influence on American fiction, but he falls too comfortably back on fashionable intellectual cliché when he ascribes this influence to "the

 shock, guilt, hatred, repugnance for country and at length plain emotional exhaustion that ruled the thoughtful young in the late sixties and early seventies." It's easy to say that Vietnam did it, or that Sirhan Sirhan did it, or that Judge Hoffman did it, and that's what has been said over and over to explain (or excuse) just about any failure on the part of the generation that came to maturity in the sixties. Obviously, these and other phenomena of the decade's political, social and cultural life must be taken into account; but in the case of writers, they are part of a rather more complex history.

For many of those writers whose work DeMott analyzes, the formative experience of the 1960s was not merely one of living through, and often participating in, political and social turmoil. Of greater importance, it was one of undergoing that turmoil in a particular place and in particular circumstances within that place. The writers whose themes DeMott characterizes as "human unresponsiveness" and "the death of fellow-feeling" were shaped by Vietnam and Kent State, to be sure, but many were even more crucially shaped by being on college campuses during the years of those traumatic events and by being students and/or instructors in creative-writing programs on those campuses.

They are, in fact, the first writing-school generation in American literary history. Previous generations of American writers were shaped by other broad influences: the frontier, World War I, the Depression, urbanization, affluence, the bomb. But to the extent that such generalizations are possible and permissible, the writers now moving into prominence are the first to have been shaped by the campus, the classroom and the professoriat. What they say in their fiction is influenced less by their own responses to events and conditions than by the responses they learned on campus. Their fiction does not, as DeMott claims, "lie in life-experience," but in attitudes to which they were conditioned in college.

If, as DeMott quite correctly points out, "middle-class youth was instructed by its elders to hide out from the draft on university campuses," then by the same token those same elders instructed it in what they regarded as the proper, orthodox way to react to events that confused and scared the student population. Anyone who spent any time on a college campus during the sixties will remember how the professors, with occasional honorable exceptions, sniffed out the first scents of rebellion and fear and quickly moved to co-opt the nascent movement by becoming more radical and even less responsible than the students themselves.

Not merely did the professors let their hair grow long, slip into blue jeans, stock up on Beatles albums and swap martinis for marijuana. They also established which attitudes were correct and which were not. The protests that the students uttered, usually in the incoherent and undisciplined language of rock lyrics, were given intellectual respectability by professors who tarted them up in the jargon of philosophy and the genres of literature. Shamelessly, the professors used their influence over the naïve and impressionable young to create a generation that left college knowing much about what the professors claimed to believe but almost nothing about how to think for itself; all the moods and attitudes legitimized by the professoriat—from alienation to marginality to narcissism to self-pity—had been learned by rote.

Nowhere were these lessons taught and learned more thoroughly than in the creative-writing departments, many of which were themselves products of the sixties and the federal education dollars that poured forth during the decade. More than most college departments, they operated then (as many do now) on the guru theory of instruction. A department's faculty might consist of no more than two or three "stars"—which often meant nothing more than that they'd published a few stories in the quarterlies—and its curriculum might consist almost entirely of courses in which students sat at the feet of these stars, submitted writing for their approval, and swallowed whole their viewpoints as well as, if the word is not too grand, their philosophies.

What came out of these departments wasn't so much a generation of writers as a generation of clones. They had soaked up all the approved fictive techniques and all the approved attitudes, and they wrote stories and novels that said all the approved things. The "life-experience" upon which these apprentice writers drew had very little to do with the real world, unless one's definition is sufficiently loose so as to admit classroom discussions, protest marches and pot parties, and a great deal to do with vicarious experience. If the fiction so many of them write is technically artful but sullen in tone and thematically empty, it's because these are the skills and attitudes that the gurus taught them.

If they'd been actively engaged in the world then instead of inhabiting the hothouse of academia, the fiction they're writing now would be very different; one need only read the novels by men who fought in Vietnam to see how writers of the same generation can produce work that, however flawed, has life and energy and originality. But originality, of course, is precisely what the writing schools are *not* about, since all but the rarest of them encourage the students to emulate the gurus, to embrace the orthodoxy of the classroom. It is this orthodoxy, rather than any genuine reaction to "life-experience," that explains the narrowness and "impassivity" of those writers whose shortcomings DeMott bemoans.

An American Master

August 20, 1984

The expenditure of public funds for the private benefit of individual artists and writers gets precious little applause in this space, but every policy—like every rule—is made to be broken. The National Endowment for the Arts has ponied up twenty-five thousand dollars to honor Peter Taylor as a "senior fellow," and the person you hear clapping is me; for the first time within recent memory, my tax dollars are going precisely where I'd put them myself.

Taylor is one of four writers thus honored; the others are Stanley Kunitz and William Meredith, the poets, and Richard Yates, the novelist. According to Frank Hodsoll, chairman of the endowment, these "senior fellowships" are intended "to support and honor creative writers and other literary professionals who have received the highest critical acclaim, but whose work may not be widely known outside the literary field." Taylor, as the most widely unknown distinguished writer in the United States, certainly fits that description.

By a coincidence that borders on the eerie, news of Taylor's selection for this honor reached me just as I was preparing to write a column about . . . Peter Taylor. This plan was occasioned by the arrival, unannounced and utterly unexpected, of a handsome new hardcover edition of Taylor's first and only novel, *A Woman of Means.* Originally published in 1950, the book had been out of print for years and only rarely appeared in rare-book catalogs; now it has been republished by the firm of Frederic C. Beil, in an elegant red binding and glassine wrapper.

For Beil, getting *A Woman of Means* back into circulation is a labor of love. His three-year-old firm has specialized up to now in books about printing, bookmaking and publishing, and *A Woman of Means* is his first purely literary venture. He has undertaken it because after reading the novel not long ago, he felt strongly that it should be generally available. Upon winning Taylor's permission, he had the book completely reset (in an exceptionally pleasing, readable typeface) and now has issued a modest first run of a couple thousand copies.

It was only a year ago that a similar effort on Taylor's behalf was made by an even younger publishing house. In June of 1983, the firm of Carroll & Graf chose as one of the books on its first list Taylor's most recent (1977) collection of short stories, *In the Miro District,* which it published as a trade paperback in a five-thousand-copy printing. To date sales have been disappointing—somewhere in the neighborhood of three thousand—and the firm finds itself in the position of being proud to publish Taylor but frustrated that it has been unable to widen his readership. Recently (just to compound the coincidence) a letter from Kent Carroll, cofounder of the firm, said: "We continue to seek and receive critical mentions of Peter Taylor's book and they are always, at the least, admiring. Yet the sales 'curve' continues to be disappointingly flat. I remain mystified as to why a writer this good (and accessible) does not capture what one would assume to be his natural audience (not to mention the readership he deserves). Perhaps the new book will break him through."

The "new book" is *The Old Forest and Other Stories,* which Dial will publish early next year, but the chances that it will provide a "breakthrough" for Taylor are singularly slender. It is a great injustice, one of the most shameful in American literary history, but Taylor seems fated to a small readership. To be sure it is a sophisticated, knowledgeable readership, and one whose loyalties range from the ardent to the fanatical, but its size is utterly inappropriate to Taylor's accomplishment. Quite simply, there is not a better writer of fiction now at work in the United States; that so few Americans are aware of this—that Taylor goes unknown and unread while vastly inferior writers perch on magazine covers, win prizes and chat up the talk shows—is a national embarrassment.

It's easy enough to explain, though. The most important reason for the neglect to which Taylor has been subjected throughout his long career is that he persists in writing short stories rather than novels; notwithstanding the vogue currently enjoyed by the literary short story, it is through novels that American writers acquire followings and reputations. Even *A Woman of Means,* Taylor's sole concession to the American yearning for bigness, scarcely qualifies as a novel; it runs no more than thirty thousand words and fills a book only through the generous application of white space.

Not merely does Taylor insist on writing stories, but he takes a long time to write them and new ones appear at frustratingly long intervals—and when they do appear, it is as often in obscure literary journals as in *The New Yorker,* where his work has found its widest readership. A couple of times in the past two or three decades Taylor has in effect vanished for several years, turning his attention to experiments in other literary forms or to the real-estate ventures that are among his principal amusements. Readers waiting for a "new Taylor" must be prepared to wait a long time, which is not calculated to encourage a mass readership.

Still, it remains an unfathomable mystery that so many thousands of literate Americans—people who read books and pay more than passing attention to literary affairs—not merely have never read Taylor but have never *heard* of him. In no way is he a reclusive or inaccessible writer; his tone is amiable and conversational, his prose is seamless and inviting, his subject matter—the domestic life of the middle class—is intimately familiar to the very Americans who form the nonacademic readership. Yet by contrast with another chronicler in short stories of middle-class life, the late John Cheever, to whose work his is in almost every respect superior, Taylor is to all intents and purposes a complete unknown.

Which is, in a word, preposterous. Rereading *A Woman of Means,* as I did recently, I was struck once again by Taylor's mastery—no other word will do—not merely of structure and style but of psychology. Not since Taylor's great hero, Henry James, has an American writer so fully understood the workings of the human mind and so effectively transformed that understanding into fiction. In *A Woman of Means,* as in virtually everything else Taylor has written, the reader is transported into a place so faithfully similar to the real world, yet so imbued with a knowledge of it few of us can hope to possess, that one is left breathless with admiration. Indeed there is no living American writer whose work I admire so much as Taylor's, and each time I read him I am forcibly reminded of how much everyone else is missing.

The Literature of Timidity

September 24, 1984

Many years ago William Faulkner, in what he subsequently called "a more or less idle remark," ranked himself and four of his contemporaries as follows, in descending order: Thomas Wolfe, Faulkner, John Dos Passos, Erskine Caldwell and Ernest Hemingway. Thereafter he spent a fair amount of time attempting to explain away both the high ranking to Wolfe and the low one to Hemingway. One such explanation was made at the University of Virginia, where he was serving as writer-in-residence, in 1957:

". . . I made my estimate on the gallantry of the failure, not on the success or the validity of the work. It's on the gallantry of the effort which failed. In my opinion, my work has all failed, it ain't quite good enough, which is the only reason to write another one, because writing really ain't any fun, I mean the mechanics of putting the stuff down on paper is no fun, I can think of too many other things I'd rather do. . . .

"I meant only that Hemingway had sense enough to find a method which he could control and didn't need or didn't have to, wasn't driven by his private demon to waste himself in trying to do more than that. So, he has done consistently probably the most solid work of all of us. But it wasn't the splendid magnificent bust that Wolfe made in trying to put the whole history of the human heart on the head of the pin, you might say."

Faulkner's was a romantic view of the novelist's mission, to be sure, even a sentimental one; but there was a real nobility in the high expectations he placed on himself and his fellow writers, in the conviction that the writer owed it to himself to push as far as he could go, to say as much as there was in him to say. Today, though, anyone who has paid close attention to American fiction of recent vintage can only find his words anachronistic; they express an ambition that seems hardly to exist any more among American writers, that seems to have disappeared along with the desire to write the once-mythical Great American Novel.

This thought came to mind repeatedly these past couple of months as I read my way through a representative selection of "serious" American fiction published between November of 1983 and October of 1984. This reading was done, with two other judges, in conjunction with a literary award that will be handed out later this fall; it was a surprisingly depressing experience. This is not to say that we encountered no good books; all of us are pleased with the three we have put on the "short list" for the award, and each of us had one or two others he'd like to have included on that list. But the absence of literary ambition in the books we read—ambition, that is, as Faulkner defined it—was startling, even to someone who reads novels for a living.

Reading these books certainly brought home the truth of an observation made by Richard Locke a few weeks ago. Reviewing the new novel by the Peruvian writer Mario Vargas Llosa, *War of the End of the World*, in *The Washington Post Book World*, Locke wrote: ". . . even in translation it overshadows the majority of novels published here in the past few years. Indeed, it makes most recent American fiction seem very small, very private, very gray, and very timid." Absolutely. It's the Latin Americans who are taking the risks these days, and in different ways the Eastern Europeans; it's the Americans, almost without exception, who are playing it safe.

It's not merely that so many American novels by "literary" writers are short; the length of a work of fiction has little to do with its depth or thematic ambition, as *The Great Gatsby* so brilliantly demonstrates. Rather, it's that the authors of these novels seem to be bending over backward to avoid large subjects and broad canvases; instead of attempting to embrace the world, they shrink into themselves. Most certainly there are writers now at work in this country who have the talent to carry off a work such as Dos Passos's *U.S.A.* or Dreiser's *Sister Carrie*, but it is just about impossible to imagine any of them doing so.

Dos Passos, Dreiser, Frank Norris, Sinclair Lewis, Wolfe—for better or worse (and sometimes worse was downright terrible) these writers reached out to their country, tried to identify and portray the national experience, filled their stories with life and energy. Their pursuit of the Great American Novel was silly and naïve, yet it encouraged them to take risks: not the precious little stylistic "risks" now so popular among our self-reverential avant-garde, but big risks that might leave them looking foolish or ignorant or inept. *U.S.A.* reverberates with risk from first page to last; in what's published now, there's scarcely a quiver.

A half century ago American writers, in the first blinding burst of a modern American literature, tried nothing less than to compress all of America between the covers of a book. To read Dreiser or Norris now, after inhabiting the thin air of Renata Adler or Joan Didion, is to be plunged into something that bears a startling resemblance to *life.* So what if the prose lumbers and lurches from time to time? The energy, the consuming interest in people and their lives, are infinitely more rewarding than the studied prose of a wan literary poseur.

To be sure, all of this grabbing for the brass ring produced some inelegant, even sloppy, books, but they were books that Americans actually read—that we still read—with what Edmund Wilson called the shock of recognition. Can anyone honestly say that of *God Knows*, Joseph Heller's latest exercise in witless stand-up comedy, or *Tough Guys Don't Dance*, Norman Mailer's cynical little potboiler, or *The Witches of Eastwick*, John Updike's precious little joke? That anyone could is exceedingly difficult to imagine—yet these three novels were far from uncharacteristic of the lot offered to our group of judges as the best that American writers of fiction had to offer in the past year.

In the end we got lucky. We found three books whose authors actually took risks—small ones, by comparison with what Faulkner attempted in *The Sound and the Fury* or Dreiser in *An American Tragedy*—but honorable books that all three judges admire. Small risks, that is, but large by comparison with everything else in the competition; at this hour in our history, ours is the literature of timidity and self-infatuation, and thus a literature in danger of exterminating itself.

"The Novelist's Real Job"

April 15, 1985

These are the words of an American reader: "I haven't read a good book in ages. I mean the literary stuff, not the junk. There's no weight to any of it. No world view. Just one more novel about some guy's mid-life crisis, or how lonely some writer is now that he's famous, or some woman rediscovering marriage for the Eighties, or that horrible metafiction where we're supposed to be thrilled because the writer can really use words!"

That reader is quoted in a piece called " 'Sensibility' and the Novel" that was published the other day in *Publishers Weekly.* It was written by Robert Ward, the author of an admirable new novel called *Red Baker,* and it aches with passion and outrage. "There are a million people coming through the creative-writing programs," Ward writes, "and all of them can sling words, but where is their spirit, their will to engage things outside their narrow little class of friends?" The central question that Ward poses is one that more and more serious readers seem to be asking:

"What happened to writers who had a really larger vision of the world, who went into the real world and observed how other people lived—authors like George Orwell, Richard Wright, adventurers like Henry Miller, bold artists like Theodore Dreiser, even Dickens and DeFoe? Writers who were able to submerge their precious selves into the difficult but rewarding task of creating characters who were *unlike* themselves. Writers, like Tolstoy, who took real chances and understood that personal fates were tied up with great historical moments. Writers who wrote passionately, and compassionately, about the poor, who had a sense of injustice as well as a sense of mystery. . . ."

What happened, Ward argues on the strength of his own experience, is that literature, and the people who make it, became divorced from life. He tells about his education at a state teachers' college where well-meaning professors of English—whom he readily credits with helping him discover his vocation as a writer—"hammered home one lesson over and over again, and that was this: the highest literary ideal was the cultivation of sensibility, and the highest sensibility one could aspire to was that of the Ironic View of Life."

Ward tried to do as he was taught, but somehow the lesson didn't take. The sixties came along and, with them, "hope and a feeling of love in the air." Gradually he learned—he may have been the only student in the sixties to do so—"how to listen all over again, not to the language of professors but that of working people." He learned that "one can write about the so-called average man with all the passion and intelligence (and even some of the irony) with which one can write about the genteel life; that poor people aren't less complex, they simply have less money."

This is a valuable lesson, and it led Ward to write a valuable book. *Red Baker* is the story of a steelworker in Ward's own home town of Baltimore who is laid off from his job at the mill around which the entire life of his neighborhood has revolved for decades; he finds himself confronted with a future that is both more complex and more mysterious than anything he has ever known, and with the certain prospect that the world in which he has lived all his life—the world he had always assumed to be immutable—will never again be the same. It is a novel about men and women (and children, too) who almost never appear in American fiction these days, yet who are heartbreakingly real and whose voices urgently need to be heard.

It's a novel about the predicament of the poor—or, more precisely, the newly poor—yet it is not a political novel. There's a reference or two in it to Ronald Reagan and the economic injustices of the early eighties, but these are comments such as one would expect to hear in ordinary conversation among ordinary people. The book is about people, not politics, and it gains much of its strength from the honesty and compassion with which it portrays them. In so doing Ward has accomplished what he describes in his essay as "the novelist's real job: creating a fictional world that reflects true, lived experience."

This is in contrast to the poor, or the lower middle class, as they customarily appear in contemporary American fiction. Such appearances are most infrequent, but when they occur it is almost always to assist the writer in grinding one or another of his own axes; these aren't characters who exist for their own worth as human beings, but caricatures who permit the author in question to express the many complaints he holds against American society. Thus, for example, we have Bob Dubois, the protagonist of Russell Banks's *Continental Drift*, a novel much overpraised in literary circles. Dubois, who in the book's early pages shows potential to be interesting and sympathetic, quickly degenerates into a mere vehicle through which Banks unloads the full arsenal of English-department political grievances, and the novel soon collapses into something not much more elevated than a political tract.

The difference between *Red Baker* and the so-called literary novels is that the former subsumes its political convictions into its characters and story while the latter sacrifice character and story to politics. The result is that the literary novels are not really about the poor or lower middle class at all; they are about elite perceptions of those classes, and elite notions about what got them into the fixes in which they find themselves. *Red Baker*, on the other hand, may well contain a substratum of political commentary—though if it does, Ward has managed to disguise it most effectively—but this is quite incidental to the powerful human story the novel tells, a story that takes its "ordinary" people seriously and that grants them the dignity they possess in actual life.

 By contrast with the work of Dickens or Dreiser, *Red Baker* is admittedly slight; its canvas is small and its themes are relatively modest. But at a time when "serious" American literature has become self-infatuated and irrelevant to the real world in which readers live, it reminds us that the door to this world is still open to writers—that all they need is the courage to walk through it. What they find when they do so will seem quite different from the world of the writing departments, but it could prove to be the raw material for fiction that, like *Red Baker*, has something to say about life as the rest of the country actually lives it. On the evidence of recent literary history, though, here's a word of caution: Don't hold your breath.

The Cult of the Self

March 31, 1986

In the peculiar world of literary publicity a few writers have acquired an aura of mystery as a result of determined if not obsessive reclusiveness: B. Traven vanishing into the Mexican wilderness, J. D. Salinger fending off *paparazzi* at his isolated New England fastness, Thomas Pynchon disappearing into parts unknown. But there can be no disputing that though these people have achieved a certain extra-literary notoriety, they are also bona fide writers whose accomplishments cannot be taken lightly.

What, by contrast, are we to make of a writer who is famous—"famous," that is, in the little world of the literati—primarily for not publishing his work? Such a fellow is Harold Brodkey, who in 1958 brought out a volume of stories called *First Love and Other Sorrows* and who has not, to all intents and purposes, been heard from since. From time to time over the years he has published snippets from a work in progress, and from time to time his publisher has listed that work, *Party of Animals,* in its catalog, but the book itself has yet to appear.

But in the literary world, especially that part of it quartered in Greenwich Village and the Upper West Side, Brodkey is a lion. Excited whispers carry the latest rumors of Brodkey's progress—a new paragraph, perhaps?—from salon to salon; breathless bulletins in the literary journals announce the prospective appearance of yet another excerpt from the "long-awaited" masterpiece, as the novel has been characterized by some who have not, in fact, actually read the whole thing.

As best as can be determined, the novel's principal subject is Harold Brodkey. He said as much recently in a long interview with the *Washington Post,* during the course of which he allowed that shaping and reshaping this fictional exploration of himself was so demanding and fulfilling a task that he simply cannot let the manuscript go. This declaration came to the attention of another writer, one who actually publishes her work. After mulling it over for a while she sent along her reaction, which I take the liberty of quoting in full:

"What about this Brodkey? Is he as wonderful as I imagine from the *Post*'s article? Can I extrapolate his whole style from so few lines? The resonance is quite stunning, don't you think? Can you imagine all the writers and would-be writers who will spend long hours lying on couches and producing horrendously dull and obscure contemplations of their own lives? Perhaps it is best not to dwell on it.

"It seems to me that by the very definition of his task, Mr. Brodkey will never finish. For if he is devoted to pounding the moments of his life for each note up and down the scale of memory, he has found undoubtedly how time changes the music of our souls by taking on a drumroll here, a string progression there, the angry blat of an off-key horn until childhood's simple melody swells into a symphony that can finish only with death!

"Well, I was pretty sure that I would like to listen to whatever pieces of the score Mr. Brodkey can bear to publish and I wondered if you shared my enthusiasm."

Nicely, and tartly, stated. My correspondent has put her finger squarely on a characteristic of modern writing that is steadily sapping the vitality from it: the pervasive, obsessive preoccupation with self. Harold Brodkey may or may not be in the process of producing a modern masterpiece—if he is, more power to him—but his unabashed self-preoccupation and self-promotion are paradigmatically contemporary. There are many reasons why modern literary fiction no longer seems pertinent to the lives of serious general readers, but surely its solipsism—its relentless self-exploration, self-flagellation and self-celebration—

is among the most important; a writer who is interested only in himself, after all, is saying in effect that he is not interested in the reader.

This self-absorption is one aspect of contemporary fiction's rebellion against the Victorian novel, which was passionately interested in everyone and everything. It can be traced directly to three overpowering influences: Joyce, who made the artist himself a legitimate subject for fictional inquiry; Proust, who turned self-scrutiny into a lifetime's occupation; and Freud, who (somewhat unwittingly) made self-analysis the avocation of the educated classes. The effect of these giants on modern literature has been staggering; the exception to today's rule is that writer—Graham Greene, Eudora Welty, William Boyd, Anne Tyler—who does *not* focus on himself.

A clear distinction should be drawn between autobiographical influence and self-preoccupation. The former is inescapable, not merely for the young writer who has little experience beyond himself—hence the characteristically autobiographical first novel—but for the experienced writer as well; everything he writes is in a sense a psychological and intellectual autobiography, even if it does not touch directly on himself. It is impossible to separate the artist from the art, and silly to try.

But self-preoccupation is another matter altogether. It is an inherently narrow view of the world, an inability to see beyond the self into the lives and minds of others. The most preternaturally gifted writer now in his prime in America may well be Philip Roth, yet his failure to move outside himself or his own experience—which seems, on the evidence he presents, to have been primarily literary and sexual—has rendered his fiction increasingly cramped and narcissistic. He repeatedly denies that his work is autobiographical, but that is not the point; he may be writing pure fiction but he is also, no matter how you slice it, writing solely about Philip Roth.

Roth deserves special mention not in order to single him out but because his gift is so prodigious and because it is so frustrating to watch him fritter it away on navel gazing. The man who could write a modern *Vanity Fair* has chosen instead to write *The Professor of Desire*, and the loss is ours. But others, less gifted than he, have been no less self-absorbed. Thomas Wolfe thought he was the world incarnate and spent his entire life exploring it; Ernest Hemingway's central character was always Ernest Hemingway, whatever the name or guise he took; novels much admired in contemporary literary circles, such as Elizabeth Hardwick's *Sleepless Nights* and Renata Adler's *Speedboat*, are little more than interior monologue masquerading as fiction.

As for Brodkey, the jury must stay out until all the evidence is in, and as my correspondent suggests, that day may never come. Not merely is there the temptation to fiddle endlessly with his self-inquiry, there is also the apprehension that a book around which he has encouraged such high expectations to collect may not fulfill them. What seems certain, though, is that if ever we are permitted to read *Party of Animals* we will learn everything we ever wanted to know about Harold Brodkey, and then some.

It's a Hell of a Town

May 26, 1986

It was enough to make the heart stop for a moment, and then sink. The mail brought a new novel by a young writer who has been laboring to notable effect in a small town about fifty miles from nowhere, writing away at books that capture the life of his region's countryside with extraordinary humor and verisimilitude. The press release accompanying the book boasted of these accomplishments, and then closed with these words: "He is presently living in New York."

No, it wasn't the misuse of "presently" that produced cardiac arrest, it was the "living in New York." What on earth has possessed the fellow? If there is a place in the United States less conducive to the writing of serious fiction than New York City generally and the Borough of Manhattan specifically, that place has escaped my attention. This writer probably is too gifted, his imagination already too richly stocked with stories and characters, to be burned out by residence in New York; but in moving there, he certainly has put his career at risk.

In moving there he has also paid homage to an old American tradition. For about a century, it has been assumed that part of a would-be author's literary rites of passage is residence in New York, preferably in its Bohemian quarters. The ritual requires that the young writer walk the streets that Howells and Wharton walked, drink where Cummings and Dos Passos drank, eat where Thurber and White ate. In New York, tradition has it, a writer thrives on the company of other writers and establishes himself in literary circles.

The only problem is that the tradition long ago expired, the victim of changes in Manhattan that make the city inhospitable to serious writers of fiction. Although a good case can be made that any young person who is ambitious and curious should have a period in New York—it is still, for all its faults, our greatest and most dynamic city—no one should suffer under the illusion that it is any longer a good place to write fiction, if, indeed, it ever was. The young writer who wants a New York period should enter it with one commitment in mind: Keep it short.

This was probably just as true in the much-sentimentalized days of Fitzgerald, Wolfe and Hemingway as it is now. Of those three writers, only Wolfe spent significant amounts of writing time in Manhattan, and he seems to have been drawn there less by the borough's literary charms than by his affair with Aline Bernstein and his dependency upon Maxwell Perkins. Hemingway was rarely more than a visitor to New York, and Fitzgerald did considerably more drinking than writing there; both did most of their work in other places, as serious novelists still do.

The evidence proves the point. Writers who serve their apprenticeships in New York escape from it almost as soon as they can. Cheever, Styron, Updike, Doctorow—they and countless others may have started out in Manhattan, but once their reputations were established they got out, presumably because they preferred places with more quiet and less hype. Louis Auchincloss remains in New York, but he has a law practice there; so too does Laurie Colwin, but she began her career in publishing and retains close ties to that industry—and in any event Manhattan is her principal subject, a statement that can be made about surprisingly few American writers of serious fiction.

In fact, New York is the setting for fewer accomplished works of fiction than many other far smaller and less celebrated cities. When I was asked last year to draw up a list of American cities that have been memorably depicted in novels or short stories, I had no difficulty with Boston, Chicago, Kansas City, Los Angeles, Memphis and New Orleans, but New York drew a blank. *Invisible Man*, perhaps, or *Manhattan Transfer*, but neither of those pins the city down, locates its essential character, the way *The Late George Apley* dissects Boston, *Studs Lonigan* encapsulates Chicago, *A Confederacy of Dunces* nails down New Orleans.

This is one of the true curiosities of American literature, one little remarked upon and not readily susceptible to explanation. Perhaps the problem is that New York is too diverse, too complex, too elusive to yield anything more than small segments of its society to the novelist; perhaps it is because American writers seem most comfortable and productive when they are writing about home, and New York may be more of a home than its native sons and daughters can cope with imaginatively. Whatever the case, you could teach a college course about the literature of Chicago (please don't!), but reading material for a study of New York wouldn't occupy anything close to a semester.

It is odd but true: The ostensible literary capital of the United States is not a city in which writers flourish. It is a grand place for journalists—there probably are more first-class ones in New York than anywhere else in the world—and also for scholars and critics; for editors and publishers, of books and magazines alike, it is absolutely essential. But with only the rarest of exceptions, for writers of fiction it is pure poison, and the young novelist from the provinces who has recently moved there is likely to find that out in a hurry.

This is because for all its receptivity to and sponsorship of literature and the arts, New York provides the wrong atmosphere for them. It may be the place that publishes their work, but it is not the place for that work to be done. New York is all hustle and bustle, wheeling and dealing, and never more so than now, when the city's emblematic figure is Donald Trump and the money changers are everywhere in charge. The point was vividly (if perhaps inadvertently) emphasized a few months ago by an article in *The New York Times Magazine* that characterized Manhattan's "new" Bohemia as far less interested in art than in commerce, a place where painters and sculptors are as shamelessly on the make as the loathsome new breed of Wall Street traders.

Worst of all for the writer is what passes, in Manhattan, for a literary community. It is not really a community of writers at all, but one of editors, publishers, reviewers, journalists and hangers-on. Its membership includes many charming and gifted people, as well as the usual—perhaps somewhat larger than usual—representation of poseurs and grifters. But it is less interested in writers' work than in their presence as literary celebrities, so the attentions it lavishes upon them are grand for the ego but devastating to the creative process. It turns writers into personalities, which means that sooner or later they stop being writers.

So go home, young writer, go home. Or at least go to New Jersey.

“The Red-Hot Center”

July 27, 1987

Somewhere in the course of its exceedingly checkered history *Esquire* magazine fashioned a mascot for itself. He was a jolly little cartoon chap in tweeds, sporting a bristly moustache and a slightly raffish look, and the magazine christened him Esky. As the bunny was for *Playboy*, Esky was meant to be the embodiment of all things *Esquire:* a gentleman of mature refinement and culture, with a bit of a British air, but also a rakish fellow who knew how to knock a few back and to give the girls—especially those drawn by Vargas—a good time.

But the times have changed. Esky has been relegated to a nearly invisible corner of the magazine's contents page; if you weren't looking for him, you'd never find him. *Esquire* has gone on to newer if not perhaps better things, and a gent of middle years such as Esky does not fit into the magazine's scheme. *Esquire* has saved itself from extinction by crafting itself into the how-to-magazine for the ambitious young, and in the universe of the yuppies there is no room for Esky, redolent as he is of times gone by.

"Man at His Best" is what *Esquire* calls itself now. Though it pays lip service to the memory of Arnold Gingrich and Ernest Hemingway and other Neanderthals who once haunted its pages, *Esquire* has moved on from aggressive masculinity to masculine "style." Its pages are now filled with advertisements for chic fashion designers (Alexander Julian, Perry Ellis, Giorgio Armani), audiovideo equipment to purchase "when you've arrived," the usual run of overpriced liquors and liqueurs, the "privileges" of "membership" in American Express, auto sound systems, exercise clothing, and—in prime position—the obligatory BMW.

Among these advertisements for the accouterments of the discreetly ostentatious life is one touting the pleasures of Rose's Lime Juice, "the uncommon denominator." This photograph has appeared in other magazines, but it seems especially comfortable in *Esquire,* the August issue in particular. It shows Arthur Schlesinger, Jr., at ease in your basic book-lined study, glass in hand, while standing atop the desk beside him, glass also in hand, is Tama Janowitz. "And so they met," the copy advises us, "the chronicler of the historical and the chronicler of the hysterical. And the word was Rose's. Splashed liberally in a vodka and tonic, and a diet cola."

The cynicism of all parties to this advertisement scarcely demands comment, but *Esquire* doesn't quit with that. March on a few pages and we arrive at "*Esquire*'s Guide to the Literary Universe," an exercise in rankmanship that seems designed as a guide, for the culturally uninitiated but acquisitive, through contemporary American literature. It is a curious document, one that takes a view both wide-eyed and cynical of "the literary world" and that in the process manages to reduce that world to little more than a sordid place where money, publicity and notoriety are held dear while art and character are valueless.

WHO'S WHO IN THE COSMOS is the headline across a three-page representation of "the literary universe," at the heart of which is something called "The Red-Hot Center." In it are listed eleven people who, according to the accompanying text, "are producing enormous amounts of heat." Appropriately enough, only five and a half of them are writers, for the literary world of *Esquire* is one in which editors and agents and hostesses have as much influence as processors of words.

"The Red-Hot Center," like the rest of *Esquire*'s map, pays lip service to the American literary establishment (Bellow, Mailer, Updike) but is primarily occupied by the gurus of "new work," which translates as yuppie fiction of the sort that happens to be prominently featured in the pages of *Esquire.* Inasmuch as *Esquire* regards it as "positive" news that "there is hardly a university in the country that doesn't have a flourishing writing program," it can come as no surprise that its map of "the literary universe" is dominated by the alumni of these programs and the people who promote their work; it is no surprise, but it surely is a dolorous comment on the state of "the literary universe."

Not all of the people on this map are chroniclers of the young and privileged and self-obsessed; draw up a list of two or three hundred people who write or publish and you are bound to rope in a few serious ones, as indeed *Esquire* has. But naming names is not, at least so far as this "literary universe" is concerned, what really matters. Though *Esquire* itself is infatuated with names—ranking them, dropping them, flaunting them—the names actually mean a lot less than what, in sum, they say.

Which is, quite simply, that contemporary American literature is precisely as shallow as the upper-middle-class American culture from which, in the main, it springs. What *Esquire* has drawn up is not so much a ranking of writers and publishers as one of hustlers and promoters. In part, needless to say, the fault and the explanation lie with *Esquire* itself, the editors of which choose to see writing and publishing in such cynical and frivolous terms; but those, alas, by and large are the terms in which writing and publishing—of so-called "literary" fiction, that is—are now practiced.

It is quite possible, of course, that the readers to whom this "Who's Who in the Cosmos" is directed will find *Esquire*'s standards of literary importance and influence entirely congenial. People whose highest goals in life are the acquisition of products and "personal style" that advertise their status are unlikely to recognize that they are being offered nothing except a guide to the valueless, since they have no standards by which to measure true worth. But what a pity it is that the current editors of a magazine that from time to time has possessed something approximating taste can come up with an overview of contemporary American literature that is little more a celebration of the shoddy and the evanescent.

No doubt it is churlish of me to write as I do, inasmuch as I have been allocated my own appropriately small satellite in *Esquire*'s "literary universe." On the whole, though, this seems not among the highest of honors that life, in its infinite capriciousness, can bring. A few of my friends also have their own little satellites, so perhaps we can go off together and start afresh; as e. e. cummings once wrote, "listen: there's a hell/of a good universe next door; let's go." When we get there we will find no red-hot center, but a few quiet corners where people can go about the singularly unglamorous business of writing and publishing and reading serious books. Perhaps we will find Esky there, too, a blonde on his arm and a glass in his hand, dreaming dreams of Papa and toasting the days that were.

The Brat Pack

October 12, 1987

It's been a bad autumn for the Brat Pack. New novels by two of its most prominent members, Bret Easton Ellis and Tama Janowitz, have been received with resounding and apparently unanimous critical disdain. More to the point, there is little evidence that either novel has made a success in the bookstores—and commercial success, above all else, is what the Brat Pack is all about.

The term refers to a small group of writers, aged thirty or considerably under, who hang out in Manhattan and have been the recipients of lavish publicity. Apart from Ellis and Janowitz, the most prominent members of the clan are Jay McInerney and David Leavitt. What all four have in common is that their first (or, in Janowitz's case, second) books were praised far out of proportion to their actual merits and sold uncommonly well for fiction by unknown writers.

These premature successes made the young authors celebrities in the tiny, self-referential world of New York publishing. At an age when most people are struggling away at entry-level jobs, these hotshots were the subjects of adulatory magazine and newspaper articles, of fawning attention at publishing cocktail parties, of fierce and expensive competition among editors and agents.

It wasn't precisely much ado about nothing, but it was close. The books that brought the four to public attention were far more notable for the timeliness of their subjects than for the manner in which the authors treated them. McInerney (*Bright*

Lights, Big City) and Janowitz (*Slaves of New York*) wrote about the glitzy, druggy new directions toward which Manhattan's journalistic and artistic community has moved in recent years; Ellis (*Less Than Zero*) wrote about the similarly glitzy and druggy world of privileged teenagers in Los Angeles; and Leavitt (*Family Dancing*) wrote about homosexuality.

In each case the writer had the good fortune to be the first to treat material for which, it seems, a ready-made readership existed—a readership eager for books about its own culture or, alternatively, a readership looking for books about a culture with which it was unfamiliar and about which it wanted to learn. The most vivid case in point was *Less Than Zero,* which was published when its author was barely twenty years old. As a work of fiction it was artless at best, but as a portrait of the pampered children of lotusland it had a devastating aura of authenticity. Younger people may have read it for titillation, but their parents read it as a disturbing report from an unknown country.

Less Than Zero did well, as did *Bright Lights, Big City, Slaves of New York* and *Family Dancing;* each author had located, and touched, a responsive chord, and each was in turn rewarded with the kind of success that most other writers can only dream about. Being young, enthusiastic and impressionable, the authors rode that success for all it was worth. To varying degrees, they became collaborators in their own lionization: Janowitz rented herself out for an advertisement, for example, and McInerney became so familiar a subject for photographic immortalization that *Spy* magazine said he "seems to be running a private tutorial in the Art of the Sullen, Dopey Literary Stare: How to Look Like You've Seen It All."

This was all well and good, if a touch obnoxious; the writers managed to make something of a name for themselves and to play the publicity game for all it was worth. Unfortunately, though, the Brats are children of an era in which publicity and celebrity have become indistinguishable from actual achievement, with the result that they managed to persuade themselves that because they were "famous"—fame, of course, being a relative thing—

they were also good. They insisted on being taken seriously, but they failed to produce anything genuinely serious.

Leavitt, who probably is closer to being a real writer than any of his compatriots, got no better than a mixed response to his second book, a novel called *The Lost Language of Cranes*. McInerney's second, *Ransom*, was roundly mocked. Now Ellis and Janowitz have met with similar fates. Ellis's *The Rules of Attraction* has been deservedly vilified as cynical and exploitive, and Janowitz's *A Cannibal in Manhattan* has been ridiculed as a piece of juvenilia. "I don't care what people say," Janowitz told the *Los Angeles Times*. "I just want them to buy the book." But apparently they are not buying, at least not in the numbers that Janowitz and her publisher had counted on.

There is a lesson here, and it is not merely that a successful first book is usually a tough act to follow. (In fact *A Cannibal in Manhattan* is not a new work at all, but an early one initially dismissed as unpublishable and now recycled to capitalize on its author's renown.) The important lesson is rather that early success can be a dangerous and debilitating thing, that it is no blessing at all but a curse in disguise—one that can destroy a career before it has really gotten off the ground.

The trouble with getting too much too soon is that it gives a person—a writer, an entrepreneur, a musician, an inventor, anyone at all—the sense that this is how life works, that success is one's natural due. Arriving as it does when one is short on experience and long on innocence, early success can only confirm a person in the belief that life is not especially difficult, that the check will always be in the mail no matter how perfunctory or callow the work for which it is paying.

The entirely predictable consequence is that the work becomes, in fact, perfunctory and callow. It is difficult to work seriously and carefully when you're distracted by—and gleefully preoccupied with—the bright lights of the big city. Writing in particular is a lonely business that cannot be done, or done well, unless the writer is alone. When the writer's time is taken up

 with parties and seminars and interviews and all the other paraphernalia of life in the fast lane, the work—the ostensible cause of the writer's celebrity—either doesn't get done or gets done badly. And when that happens the one certainty is that sooner or later it will catch up with the writer. The public that lionized him will figure out that he's no longer worth reading and will drop him as quickly as it applauded him.

There is nothing new about this cruel phenomenon; ask Scott Fitzgerald. But it's far more dangerous now than it was in his day, because the machinery of publicity has become so gigantic and because the money can come so easily and in such huge amounts. Nowadays you can be a college student one day and a magazine personality the next; ask Bret Easton Ellis. But as soon as you begin to mistake the noise of attention for the actuality of accomplishment, the end is in sight; the Brat Pack may think it's something new and unique, but in fact it's just playing out a very familiar story.

This Is "Racism"?

January 25, 1988

The first question is: Inasmuch as the 1988 Pulitzer prizes have yet to be awarded, why are four dozen Afro-American writers issuing a public complaint about Toni Morrison's failure to win one? The second: Are prizes really so important—"keystones to the canon of American literature"—that it is necessary to make a scene over Morrison's alleged mistreatment at the hands of those who award them? The third: Since the suggestion has been made that Morrison has failed to win a major prize because she is black, are we now to understand that she should be given one . . . because she is black?

These and any number of other questions, few of them pleasant, are raised by the two documents published in the January 24 issue of *The New York Times Book Review* and widely discussed in various other publications and broadcasts last week. The first is a somewhat hysterical letter by June Jordan and Houston A. Baker, Jr., lamenting the "shame" and "national neglect" suffered by Morrison and the late James Baldwin because of the failure of each to win either a Pulitzer or a National Book Award. The second is a "Statement" signed by these two writers and forty-six others that begins:

"Despite the international stature of Toni Morrison, she has yet to receive the national recognition that her five major works of fiction entirely deserve: She has yet to receive the keystone honors of the National Book Award or the Pulitzer Prize. We, the undersigned black critics and black writers, here assert ourselves against such oversight and harmful whimsy."

The sincerity of those who signed this statement is not open to question, nor is the dignity with which they, as black writers, "urgently affirm our rightful and positive authority in the realm of American letters." Their willingness to speak out as a group is heartening evidence of their self-esteem and their determination to be accepted, as well they should be, as legitimate contributors or aspiring contributors to American literature. But however much we may sympathize with their feelings and their desire for recognition, we must not let this blind us to the rather less attractive implications of their protest.

It comes two and a half months after the 1987 National Book Award for Fiction was presented not to Morrison's *Beloved,* one of the five finalists, but to Larry Heineman's first novel, *Paco's Story.* The decision had been reached by a two to one vote of the jury, one member of which was the prominent Afro-American novelist Gloria Naylor, whose name was conspicuously absent among the signers of the current protest. According to a report last week on public radio, Morrison was "devastated" by this disappointment; the statements in the *New York Times,* with their deeply felt praise for Morrison, appear designed as much to ease this "devastation" as to protest the "neglect" she ostensibly has suffered.

But the truth is that it's a form of "neglect" virtually any other writer would kill for. Like all of Morrison's previous novels, *Beloved* was the recipient of extravagant, indeed excessive, reviews, and it spent a number of weeks on the best-seller lists. It was a finalist for both the National Book Award and the National Book Critics Circle Award; it may well be among the three finalists recommended to the Pulitzer board by the fiction jury, though I have no inside knowledge to that effect. By any reasonable standard it has been a great success, one that Morrison and her claque should be applauding rather than bemoaning.

Yet here we have Morrison "devastated" at her failure to win an award and her admirers issuing a thinly veiled suggestion that this failure was due to racism on the part of the American literary community. Nothing could be further from the truth, and it is time to put the canard to rest once and for all. The plain fact is that over the years Morrison has if anything been the beneficiary of the literary community's good intentions. Literary people in the United States tend to be humane and liberal in outlook, if not always in practice, and to search out opportunities to express these sentiments. Morrison, who writes eloquently and powerfully about black life and history, has provided precisely such an opportunity; it has been seized over and over again by publishers, reviewers, other writers and ordinary readers.

There are millions of black Americans with ample grievances about discrimination, but at least in literary terms Toni Morrison most emphatically is not among them. She is in fact among the privileged few, not merely as a nationally celebrated author but also as an editor at one of the country's most respected publishing firms, Random House. Nobody is out to "rob" Morrison of awards. She "lost" the National Book Award not for racial reasons but because one juror felt passionately about *Paco's Story* and managed to persuade another juror to that view; she "lost" the Book Critics Circle Award (which in fact she had won a decade earlier for *Song of Solomon*) because there was stronger support within the organization's board for Philip Roth's *The Counterlife* (to which the award ultimately went) and Tom Wolfe's *Bonfire of the Vanities*.

The point is so basic that laboring it is ridiculous, but here goes anyway: It is possible to make a literary judgment without making a racial judgment as well. It is possible that two groups of judges can meet, quite independently of each other, and decide that certain books by writers who happen to be white are "better" than a certain book by a writer who happens to be black—and that their decisions can have nothing, absolutely nothing, to do with race. It is even possible that when the Great Juror in the Sky comes to make the final decision, the one for all eternity, She will decide that *Beloved* is not as good a novel as *Passion Moon Rising*, by Rebecca Brandewyne.

When it comes to judgments about books—or chocolate-chip cookies, or movies, or musical compositions—anything is possible; Toni Morrison is the victim, if that is how her admirers choose to see her, not of racism but of possibility. To suggest to the contrary is merely to muddy the waters, to raise an issue that is entirely irrelevant and to impugn the motives of honest people who tried, as best they could, to reach honest decisions under difficult circumstances.

To say this is not to deny that black writers have suffered discrimination or that some have been given insufficient recognition; certainly it is an oddity, and a literary if not racial injustice, that none of the country's most prestigious literary prizes managed to find its way to James Baldwin, though we do well to remember that in other ways he was much honored in his lifetime. But Scott Fitzgerald and Thomas Wolfe never won Pulitzers; neither did Flannery O'Connor and John Dos Passos. The giving of awards, like life itself, is imperfect, and many deserving books have gone without honor; but race has nothing to do with it, and to suggest as much is nothing except dangerous self-delusion.

Mr. Bellow's Manuscript

May 9, 1988

If you haven't anything better to do on June 7, and if your loose change is burning a hole in your pocket, why not take a trip to Manhattan? In that city on that day Sotheby's is to auction off the manuscript and related papers of Saul Bellow's novel *Mr. Sammler's Planet*. Advance guessing has it that you can take the whole package home—four notebooks in Bellow's hand, his typescript, the galley proofs—for somewhere between $60,000 and $100,000.

The guessing range is so wide because this is something that has never before been done—the public auction of an American author's private literary papers—and as a result no one really knows what the market will bear. The hunch here, though, is that the *Mr. Sammler's Planet* papers will go for close to $100,000, maybe considerably more, and that in consequence authors everywhere will begin plowing through their files for marketable memorabilia.

Mr. Sammler's Planet is anything but one of Bellow's most consequential works, but that is hardly the point. Not merely is Bellow the winner of a Nobel Prize for Literature—*Mr. Sammler* was published in 1970, and the prize came six years later—but he is arguably our most distinguished and revered living writer. Into the bargain the auction houses have been running a seller's market lately—consider, if your stomach is up to it, the Andy Warhol auctions—and Sotheby's is sure to milk *Mr. Sammler* for every nickel it can yield.

This is grand news for Sotheby's and Saul Bellow but not

so grand, some say, for the nation's scholars and librarians. The curator of one prominent library told the *New York Times* that she could understand why Bellow is disposing of the manuscript, but was concerned nonetheless. "For him it's over," she said, "but it is not over for the reader and the literary critic, and it is not over in the flow of literary history. The written traces of great creative minds will just disappear if their manuscripts do."

Similar sentiments were expressed by a curator at the Regenstein Library of the University of Chicago, where five of Bellow's earlier—and more important—manuscripts are preserved. "We made a very strenuous effort to keep the manuscript," this gentleman said, "but for reasons of his own Mr. Bellow decided to remove it. I don't think it will stop scholarship altogether. However, the literary corpus may be fragmented and that may cause various degrees of inaccessibility or inconveniences for scholars."

But is anyone shedding any tears for the poor scholars, apart from the scholars themselves and their friends in the libraries? I rather doubt it. Implicit in the words of both these curators is an assumption that writers somehow have a duty to preserve their manuscripts and other papers for "scholarship," but in fact that duty exists solely in the minds of those who stand to benefit from the exercise of it. In actuality, the only duty that writers—or any other artists—owe is to themselves and to the visions they seek to bring to life through their work.

This always has been so; only recently has the conceit been nurtured to life, within the groves of academe, that authors and artists exist primarily not to create art but to satisfy the bottomless appetite of this noble creature called scholarship. In English departments where deconstructionists and structuralists hold sway, authors are regarded with something approximating contempt; criticism, after all, matters more than that which is critiqued or the person who created it.

Several years ago it was my misfortune to fall among semioticians and other thieves at a literary symposium here in Washington. For what seemed an eternity they droned on and on, flattering each other and knifing absent colleagues, speaking the academic equivalent of glossolalia. At last one of them, a particularly smug fellow from a mediocre university in the west, stirred in his chair. "Gentlemen!" this eminence exclaimed to the accompaniment of a general hush. "One thing upon which we must agree: the United States leads the world in criticism!" This was greeted by a small rush of self-congratulatory applause, following which all adjourned for a bracing round of sherry.

It is easy to imagine how these fellows must be reacting to the news that Saul Bellow, a literary corpus if ever there was one, is about to put part of that corpus out on the market. At public sale! Doubtless to be purchased by some rich philistine who'll stow it away in his own library and won't let any scholars near it! How dreadful! What will we poor scholars do?

At the risk of sounding quite the philistine myself: tough luck. Saul Bellow understands what the academic moles do not—that *Mr. Sammler's Planet* belongs to him and him alone and is his to dispose of in whatever manner he prefers. No doubt he would say to them as well that if they want to study *Mr. Sammler's Planet*, let them study the finished and published book; that, after all, is the book that Bellow himself chose to put before the public, not the early draft or the typescript.

The scholars will respond, predictably, that from the early version of a book they can scrutinize what they like to call "the author's intentions," but in the case of a living writer the argument simply does not hold water. Certainly it is true that, for example, the published version of *Sartoris* was quite different from Faulkner's original, and preferred, manuscript; but Bellow has made no public complaints about his treatment at the hands of editors, and therefore we have no reason to believe that the early versions of *Mr. Sammler's Planet* will yield anything except minor literary curiosities.

But it is from such, alas, that scholarly careers are now made. Burrowing their way into manuscripts and typescripts, shopping lists and telephone bills, the moles emerge with the detritus from which what passes for "criticism" is manufactured. Small wonder, therefore, that they are shocked and alarmed at Bellow's precipitous action: How many dissertations may go unwritten, now that *Mr. Sammler* has been consigned to the foul world of commerce and reality?

The more the merrier, for my money—and if I had enough of it I'd buy the *Sammler* manuscript myself, for the sheer pleasure of knowing that it would thus go untouched by the moles and drones of the Modern Language Association. Indeed my only complaint with Bellow's plans has to do with how he intends to dispose of the money from the manuscript sale. "I have the thought," he says, "to endow a chair in some university for a writer." Please! Abandon that thought forthwith! Give the money to the Mafia, or Jimmy Swaggart, or the Ed Meese Defense Fund! Anything at all, so long as it's not yet another writer subsidized by the ivory tower of academia.

Grandstanding on Rushdie

February 27, 1989

For what little it is worth I am, as seems to be commonly known in certain smart circles, the "book critic for a large metropolitan newspaper" who, as a scurrilous editorial in the March 13 issue of *The New Republic* has it, "refused to review *John Dollar* by Marianne Wiggins, who is [Salman] Rushdie's wife, because a favorable review might make him a target" for the hit squads assigned to Rushdie by the Ayatollah Khomeini.

This smear, word of which was first brought to me in separate telephone calls two weeks before *The New Republic*'s editorialist gave it currency and legitimacy, is a lie. It has no foundation in fact and is the invention of persons who either were misinformed or who, for whatever reason, sought to undermine such small reputation as I enjoy. Had *The New Republic* held its editoralist to ordinary standards of journalistic responsibility and courtesy, its editorialist would have checked the rumor with me before publishing it and his or her weasel words presumably never would have been written; but checking with me would of course have involved confronting the truth, and that would have been inconvenient.

Here is the truth. The book was assigned for review by *The Washington Post Book World* weeks before the Rushdie affair, and to a reviewer (whose admiring notice appeared yesterday) other than me. Until the furor over *The Satanic Verses*—which I did review, unfavorably, long before the ayatollah's diatribe—I had been unaware that Wiggins and Rushdie were married and indeed I had not, to my present recollection and embarrassment, ever heard of her or her works. It is as simple as that; but to *The New Republic,* and others hell-bent on posturing as the beleaguered Rushdie's soulmates, brushing aside simple truth seems as easy as cranking up the editorial windbag.

The source of the rumor remains a mystery to me, at least in some of its particulars, but it's easy enough to locate the fundamental explanation for it. The American literary and publishing community has been thrown into a tizzy by the Rushdie business, and for a couple of weeks rumor seems to have become its staple diet. So, too, has recrimination, as at first people were reluctant to speak out on Rushdie's behalf but not especially reluctant to criticize others for failing to do so. Now that various literary personages have found safety in numbers and spoken out en masse, the tide of self-righteousness threatens to engulf us all.

To this tide I have no original or interesting waves to contribute. I have nothing except sympathy and—if the word is appropriately applied to a proud and self-assured man—pity for Rushdie, and I am as appalled as the next person by the "death sentence" that has been handed down on him without benefit of trial or, so far as I can determine, systematic inquiry. In the history of Western literature his case is one without precedent, and I shudder to imagine how it may be concluded.

But condemnation of those who have been fearful of rushing to his side strikes me as more an exercise in self-promotion on the part of those issuing it than a useful contribution to Rushdie's defense. The same goes for condemnation of booksellers, chains and independents alike, that have chosen any number of policies designed to reduce the possibility of violence against their employees, ranging from outright refusal to sell *The Satanic Verses* to removing the book from display and selling it only on request.

Perhaps it is all in the eye of the beholder. What to some may seem mere prudence is, to others, cowardice. But I cast my lot with prudence. As the entire brief history of this astonishing incident makes plain, we are dealing with a culture whose rules are so different from our own and whose interpretation of those rules is, in our terms, so far beyond comprehension that caution and discretion seem not merely the wisest but the only sane course. At a time when acts of terrorism have become a daily reality of global politics, to hurl oneself into the controversy without careful consideration of the consequences strikes me as, if not lunacy, foolhardy in the extreme.

For private individuals, writers and others, the decision to speak out or remain silent obviously is a personal one, with repercussions that presumably will be largely private. But for the operator of a bookstore or a chain of stores, the implications are broader and less easily assessed. Writing last week in the *New York Times,* Harry Hoffman of Waldenbooks made an articulate and persuasive case for his decision to withdraw the book from display (but not sale) in his twelve hundred stores; he did not want violence done against his employees, he said—there had been threats—and he considered this a responsible step to avert it. That he has now relaxed this policy, in effect allowing individual store managers to do as they please, is welcome; but to dismiss his earlier apprehension, or that of any other bookseller, as mere cowardice is callous, smug and self-righteous.

But smugness and self-righteousness are, alas, commonplace in certain quarters of the American literary community. While writers in England and on the Continent keep their own counsel—terrorism is a known quantity there, and circumspection seems to be held in higher regard—several in this country assembled last week in New York, under the aegis of various organizations, to declare their "solidarity," as the redoubtable Susan Sontag put it, with the beleaguered Rushdie.

Leaning against the comfortable cushion of the six thousand miles of air space separating them from the ayatollah, not to mention the police protection their meeting was afforded, these giants of American literature delivered themselves of vast emissions of wind. Rhetorical overkill was everywhere in the air, as the competition to claim the lion's share of Rushdie's reflected martyrdom intensified. The championship may have been a toss-up, between Diana Trilling ("Rushdie the individual yields place to Rushdie the symbol of our freedom to write and publish what we want") and Norman Mailer: "If he is ever killed for a folly, we must be killed for the same folly."

Perhaps all of this gave comfort to Rushdie, who sent word at week's end that he was grateful for the support his cause had attracted around the world, but as a writer with a keen eye for cant he must have been amused, if not appalled, at the facility with which these well-padded beneficiaries of American freedom and military protection wrapped themselves in the mantle of his persecution. No doubt many of the words sent his way from the PEN American Center were heartfelt and sincere, but the appropriation of Rushdie as a "symbol" of repression that does not in fact exist in this country was opportunistic and vulgar.

The truth is that if there was a brief period of uncertainty and fear in the American bookselling community, it has long since passed. It's not Harry Hoffman who's keeping *The Satanic Verses* out of the stores these days; it's Viking Penguin, Rushdie's publisher, which is struggling desperately to fill the huge back orders the book has attracted. Before long the new printing will be in hand, the book will be back in the stores, and the book community can get back to what is, in this country, the real business at hand: cashing in.

Sad it may certainly be, but it is true: Salman Rushdie in hiding from his assigned murderers has become not a symbol of freedom to write and to publish but an instrument through which others can advance, or seek to advance, their own interests. Booksellers ordering the book in vast quantities, authors and journalists showing off their devotion to the higher verities, an ayatollah trying to co-opt his more "pragmatic" underlings: Where, in all these schemes, does Salman Rushdie, the man in hiding, have any true importance?

The Lit'ry Life: II

June 19, 1989

At the stroke of midnight last Monday, my coach turned back into a pumpkin. I shook hands with Larry King, thanked him for having me on his radio program, and walked off into the night, my silent cheers soaring to the stars. After two months, I was a free man: My book tour was over.

Ah yes, the book tour. It is, to some people, the object of envy and mythification. People who write books but have never been granted the privilege of a tour assume that it is just the elixir their careers crave—that if only they could be allowed to do signings in Minneapolis and radio shows in Cleveland, their books would rocket to the upper reaches of the best-seller lists. By the same token, people who read books assume that the book tour is the ultimate in glamour, a magical-mystery express in the course of which the lucky author gets to schmooze with Johnny Carson, sip champagne in first class, and hold court in a five-room suite at the Ritz Carlton.

That is the myth. The reality, as almost anyone who has suffered through one will attest, is that a book tour is a movable torture chamber the twin purpose of which is to reduce an author to a state of quivering insanity while simultaneously proving to him, beyond the shadow of a doubt, that nothing he can say or do will persuade a single person to buy his book. A book tour is neither a pleasure ride at the publisher's expense nor a sure-fire selling device; it is, quite to the contrary, a lesson in humility from which only the most insufferably self-assured return unchastened.

That publishers underwrite book tours, much less that authors agree to undertake them, should be mysteries beyond all explanation, but in fact this is not so. Publishers send authors on tour because (a) they can cover more ground for less money with tours than with advertising and (b) they'd just as soon let authors do all the dirty work anyway. Authors hit the road because (a) they know in their hearts it's the Yellow Brick Road to their own Oz of wealth and fame and (b) they're convinced—often with very good reason—that their publishers have been asleep at the switch since publication day, so they'd better do the dirty work themselves.

It's simple: Mix a publisher's indifference with an author's vanity and—presto!—what you end up with is a book tour. It enables a publisher to show an author how much it loves him and an author to preen before newspaper reporters, bookshop customers and radio microphones. But what it does not do, at least in my all-too-sobering experience, is sell books. How books are sold is a process that defies analysis, explanation or divination; the marketing of books is presided over by the Great Bookseller in the Sky, and he isn't giving away any secrets—except to advise that if you want to sell a book, don't go on tour.

Myth has it that touring is lunch at the Four Seasons and dinner (the same day, of course) at Antoine's, but cold reality is that touring is an overbooked flight—coach, of course—to Minneapolis that bangs through thunderstorms and deposits you in the Twin Cities an hour and a half behind schedule. The flight costs $460, plus about $150 in other expenses—it would be more, except you stay with relatives—all of which seems to have been flushed down the nearest drain: Your reading at a bookstore is attended by eighteen people, ten of whom are (a) relatives, (b) friends of relatives and (c) bookstore employees. You sell a dozen books, which works out, factoring in expenses, to approximately $50 per sale; the list price of the book is $21.95.

Touring is driving from one end of North Carolina (picking up a speeding ticket along the way) for "signings," as the quaint custom is euphemistically known, in various cities. For two hours you sit behind a card table, staring bleakly into the void as customer after customer enters the store, gives you a puzzled glance, and ventures back to the greeting-card section—or, just to rub it in, walks out with a copy of precisely the book you fancy to be your competition. If you sign half a dozen books in two hours you count yourself lucky and console yourself with the thought that scarcity is bound to increase the signatures' value.

Touring is interviews in which, over and over again, evidence is provided of the truth of Yardley's Law: Newspaper interviewers have usually read your book, radio interviewers have sometimes read it, television interviewers have never read it. Can there be a more exquisite torture known to civilized man than to be forced to conduct an animated conversation, under the full heat and glare of television's lights, on a set approximately as conducive to relaxation as Torquemada's chambers, with a person who has no knowledge of the subject under discussion and no interest in acquiring such knowledge?

Touring is being driven around all day by a person called an "escort" and worrying all day about how much, if at all, that person should be tipped. Touring is racing through the airport to catch the shuttle to Boston, then sitting on the ground for half an hour before the thing takes off. Touring is a whole day in a city with only one interview on the schedule and trying to figure out how to kill the other twenty-three hours. Touring is getting to your motel and finding a message from your publisher, who "forgot" to tell you that from 6 to 8 P.M. you're supposed to be signing books, when all day you'd looked forward to a drink, the evening news, and an early bedtime. Touring is, in another city, getting to your hotel and finding another message from your publisher, this one saying that two of the day's four interviews have been cancelled.

Why are you doing all of this? Why are you further wounding an ego that's already taken a bruising from reviewers and other malefactors? Because a few months ago, in the white heat of prepublication optimism, you said to your publisher, "I'll do anything I can to help my book," and your publisher took your words at face value. How can you possibly know that the best thing you can do for your book is stay at home, stick to your knitting, and spare the rest of the world your bumbling, inarticulate explanation of its contents?

You're a fool, that's what you are, and as the man said: Experience keeps a dear school but fools will learn in no other. By the last day of the school's spring term you're sadder and wiser and all that, but mainly you're just ready to go home and get back to whatever passes for normal in your life. Thus it was that, after giving my heartfelt thanks to Larry King, I scarcely needed an elevator to get to the ground floor and my car was almost an irrelevance—I could have made it home on my own power, so relieved was I to have the tour behind me.

When I got in the car I flipped on the radio. King was saying that the postmaster general was on next and that the following evening's guest would be Russell Baker, who would talk about his new book. Hah! All I had for that piece of news was a malicious smirk. Okay, Baker, I thought, it's your baby. Better thee than me. Tour on! And while you're at it, have a nice day.

Real Men Read Books

December 4, 1989

For as long as there has been television, people in the book industry have cast wistful eyes at its flickering screen and thought: If only we could find some way to harness it to our advantage! If only we could persuade people who love TV that reading is fun, too! If only we could put on a *real* television advertising campaign, one that *works*!

So now, just in time for Christmas, that's what you'll find on TV, if you look in the right places. The other day, on the early morning and early evening news, the ad campaign for B. Dalton, the book-selling chain, made its seasonal reappearance—the answer, you'd think, to every publisher's dream. Dream on. Wouldn't you know it? Beneath its jolly promotion of books as apt seasonal gifts, the campaign has a subtler message that surely must be every book publisher's nightmare: The people who buy and read books are wimps.

No kidding, that's what it says. The spots show a variety of book jackets—children's books or best sellers, depending on which ad you happen to see—while the titles are read by a male voice that is most charitably described as mincing. Then at the end the camera cuts to a nice little fellow—in spectacles, if you can believe it—who looks for all the world like Casper Milquetoast's favorite son. He smiles sweetly at the camera and says, "You can call me 'Books.' "

We can call you a lot of other things, friend, few if any of them fit for a family newspaper. The actor portraying this chap
 no doubt is the embodiment of masculinity—he probably runs

thirty miles before breakfast and eschews the escalator in favor of the pole vault—but the character he plays is the wimp to end all wimps. The guy makes Mister Rogers look like Sylvester Stallone; he's a wimp, a nerd, a drip, a dweeb—and, if we're to believe B. Dalton, he's "Mister Books."

On Publishers' Row they must be tearing their hair. Here the industry is struggling through one of the more depressing periods in its recent history, facing innumerable and perhaps intractable difficulties, and one of the country's two largest book chains comes along with commercials that say, in so many words, that reading is for mama's boy and teacher's pet. That'll get the customers out to the bookstores, won't it?

And speaking of mama's boy, what about Papa? You know, Papa Hemingway. His grave's probably spinning so fast, it's just about to levitate. It's true, to be sure, that Papa seems to have had certain problems with his own masculinity—when he was a lad his mother liked to dress him in girls' clothes, and his posthumous novel *The Garden of Eden* contains some fairly bizarre cross-sexual stuff—but that's all the more reason for him to have been just about the most aggressively macho author in the whole history of authors.

Why, if Papa caught a glimpse of Mister Books, it's terrible to think what he might do to the poor fellow. A man who was Man enough to punch out Scott "Minnesota Mauler" Fitzgerald and Morley "Canadian Cruncher" Callaghan in the boxing ring in Paris surely would give no quarter to this nice little fellow in his granny spectacles and comfy flannel shirt. Papa would clean his clock, hang him out to dry, run him through the wringer—and strut away mumbling something like, "That'll teach the creep to mess around with a *real* reader."

Speaking of which: Has anybody told Norman about this? You know, Norman Mailer, ladies' man and pugilist extraordinaire. This is a guy who writes with his fists, so what on earth is he likely to say about a guy who reads with his pinkie? He'll probably give a quick call to John Irving: "Come on, stud, put on your wrestlin' duds, we've got a little job to do." Poor Mister

Books! He'd be better off at the tender mercies of Mike Ditka and Wilt the Stilt.

What the good folks at B. Dalton don't seem to understand is that writin' and readin' aren't for sissies; they're for mean hombres, and anyone who suggests otherwise had better be ready to pay the consequences. As the man said, "When you call me that, smile." And who was that man? He wasn't any pro football player or weight lifter or six-hundred-pound Mafioso enforcer, no sir: That man was a *writer*, name of Owen Wister. He may have come from an old Philadelphia family with antique furniture in the parlor and aunts who went to the opera, but when Mister Wister put pen to paper, the earth *moved*.

Readin's hard work—it certainly is a hell of a lot harder than watching television—and it takes a tough kind of fellow to do the job. It's like Roosevelt Grier and his needlepoint: You need a big guy to read a little book. Why, before I settle down to a day's readin'—"book critic," that's my game, and you've got to be All Man to play it—I flex my pecs a few times, just to get in proper trim, and after I've cold-cocked the dachshund and wasted the cat, I crack open the book with my teeth.

Oh, I know, lots of people associate readin' with ladies' tea clubs and cucumber sandwiches with the crust cut off and nice little twerps like Mister Books, but that's so far from the truth, it isn't even within shouting distance. You probably didn't know this, but before a guy can be in a Miller Lite Beer commercial he has to take a readin' test. Anything less than sixty words a minute, forget it; guy reads that slow, no way he can hang around with the likes of Rodney Dangerfield and Bob Uecker and . . .

And Mickey Spillane. You think they chose him to be one of the Miller guys because he looks tough and talks tough and walks tough and drinks tough? No way. They chose Mickey Spillane because they know that to anyone who grew up in the 1950s—which is to say anyone who's around fifty now, right there at prime spending time—Mickey Spillane is, well, come to think of it, someone had a name for it.

Yes. Mickey Spillane is *Mister Books*. Mickey Spillane is so hard-boiled he makes Dashiell Hammett look like wilted cabbage, and Mickey Spillane is books from top to toe. Books like *I, the Jury* and *Vengeance Is Mine* and *Kiss Me, Deadly,* and *The Big Kill* and *My Gun Is Quick* and (you'd better believe it) *Tough Guys*. Mickey Spillane may be seventy-one years old, but he's a lean, mean writin' machine, and when he isn't writin', he's readin'. Why, to Mickey Spillane knocking off a couple of volumes of Proust after dinner is about as easy as taking the dog out for a walk. He's such a mean hombre that back in the fifties, Pogo gave him an alias: Called him Mucky Spleen.

Now we call him Mister Books. So what it says here, B. Dalton, is, let's go back to production. Thanks a lot, but no thanks. Can the wimp, and while you're at it can the ad agency that came up with him. Mickey Spillane, aka Mucky Spleen, aka Mike Hammer, is the man you want. "You can call me 'Books,' " he'll say in the commercial. "And when you call me that, *smile*."

PART TWO

The American Scene

Welcome to the Club

January 17, 1983

When it comes to clubs and clubbiness, many a good fellow loses all sight of reason and descends into unwitting self-parody. Consider as a case in point the late John O'Hara, whose keen nose for the pretensions of others utterly deserted him when it came to his own towering ambition to be the ultimate clubman. Here, for example, he grovels before an acquaintance in the hope of enlisting assistance in his endeavor to scale yet another Olympus:

". . . do you still belong to the Philadelphia Racquet Club? If you do, would you consider putting me up for non-resident membership? I now belong to the Century, the Leash, the Coffee House, the Nassau Club, the Quogue Field Club, the Shinnecock Yacht Club, the National Press Club and the Beach Club of Santa Monica. . . . I have an old P.R.C. roster and I know quite a few members, but I don't think any of them would carry as much weight as you. Certainly none I'd rather have go to bat for me."

It is significant, no doubt, that O'Hara listed the Century Club first among these high honors, for membership in that august association was something for which he had labored with shameless persistence. His friendship with the playwright Philip Barry was nearly sundered by Barry's initial reluctance to put him up for the Century, out of the entirely reasonable conviction that the obstreperous O'Hara most surely would be blackballed—as in fact he was once Barry capitulated. O'Hara's biographer, Matthew Bruccoli, writes: "When Barry refused to resign from the Century in protest, O'Hara refused to speak to him for a time." At last, many years later, O'Hara was granted admission to this paradise, and remained a proud, steadfast member for the rest of his life—which granted him the privilege to grouse, in 1962, about "the number of creeps who have been creeping into the Century."

They were of course creeps of the male persuasion. One shudders to imagine how O'Hara would thunder and rage were he around to witness the move now afoot to open the Century to creeps of the female persuasion. This undertaking was reported last week in the *New York Times,* which published the texts of several documents relating to the identity crisis through which the Century is suffering—coverage such as is ordinarily accorded only to presidential news conferences and Middle Eastern wars.

On one side in this donnybrook stand the rebels, some three hundred strong, who advocate the admission of women to the Century, which was founded in 1857 for "authors, artists and amateurs of letters and the fine arts;" they describe the club as "a gathering place for cultivated people" and contend that accepting women "seems appropriate in view of our club's principles." On the other side, evidently much in the majority, stand those who treasure "the effortless, unconstrained companionship among men and the casual freedom of association which over all the years has characterized the Century," and who, need it be said, are manning the barricades against the dreaded invasion of *les gals.*

What is rather mysterious about this business is the assumption on the part of these self-described "cultivated people" that any self-respecting woman would want to join their number. There is much to be said for Groucho Marx's oft-cited observation that "I wouldn't want to belong to any club that would accept me as a member," but there is also much to be said for the logical variation thereon: Who wants to be a member of a club that does *not* want him as a member?

And why—here we really get right to the essence of it—would any woman in her right mind want to be a member of a men's club in the first place? Have any of the ladies visited one of those clubs lately? If they have, and if they still want to join, then membership is probably the fate they deserve.

There are, so far as I can tell, only four reasons to abandon one's dignity and sign on at a club: a pleasant refuge in which to sit and read, friendly and personal service, a good meal and a good drink. Yet in no men's club of my acquaintance is even one of these amenities remotely approximated. The seating in these establishments, to begin with, invariably consists of ancient chairs of immense avoirdupois in which the stuffing has gone lumpy and the leather has acquired a distinct odor of stale tobacco; the reading matter consists of last month's magazines and copies of today's newspaper from which two sections are missing and in which the crossword already has been demolished by some other geezer.

The member who lurches out of his chair and makes for the dining room or bar has in store a style of service that seems modeled after the comedy, such as it is, of Don Rickles or Phyllis Diller. One might expect, after the expenditure of many thousands in initiation fees and annual dues, a certain obsequiousness on the part of the hired help, but it is nowhere to be found. Instead, the barman gazes into space, calculatedly ignoring one's increasingly desperate signals, and the waitress slams one's food about with gestures that travel the short distance between indifference and contempt. This is perhaps as it should be, but surely it is not what the clubman bargained for.

Surely, too, he cannot have bargained for the food, though forsooth it may remind him of the fare dished out during his halcyon days at boarding school. Not long ago I dined with a friend at a noted Washington club where the powerful gather in masculine splendor to cast melancholy gazes at food that defies description. He remarked, as the waitress menaced us with the menu, that there was a standing rivalry between his club and another across town to see which can serve the least edible food; my experience—limited experience, I am glad to say—has been that the winner of this competition is whichever club I happen to be a guest in at the moment. Once, I must confess, I was served a notable lamb chop at a men's club; but this effort was nicely defeated by the cold potatoes and canned peas that accompanied it.

Then there are the drinks. Surely a chap should expect of his club—his sanctuary, his home away from home—a proper drink. But no. A clubman's bloody Mary consists of a dribble of vodka, tomato juice that has been cut generously with water, and last week's celery stalk; it is served after sitting, on ice, for several hours. As for the clubman's martini, it hardly deserves the name. Poke through the ice—poke quickly, as it's rapidly melting—and you'll find a concoction vaguely reminiscent of the notorious "martini" assembled with inexplicable pride by Franklin Delano Roosevelt, a drink the mere mention of which struck terror in the hearts of those forced to grin and bear it. FDR mixed two parts vermouth (sometimes three) to one part gin, and in his honor this is still done in clubs from Boston to San Francisco.

That these pleasures could be the aspiration of any civilized, much less "cultivated," woman, is quite beyond my ken. Surely the efforts of Steinem, Millett and Smeal have gone for something loftier—not to mention tastier—than Breaded Veal Cutlets à la St. Grottlesex.

Never-Never Land: I

May 30, 1983

No doubt the leaders of the free and industrialized world have had a high old time during their summit meeting at Colonial Williamsburg. Certainly they chose an appropriate spot for their maunderings, for the connection between Colonial Williamsburg and historical reality is approximately the same as the connection between contemporary political leadership and real life: nonexistent.

Colonial Williamsburg is the Disney World of the American past. To stroll down its meticulously groomed byways or to sup at its calculatedly chummy taverns is to disappear into a world that, our most ardent fantasies to the contrary notwithstanding, never was. For all the patina of "historical authenticity" with which Williamsburg has been fancied up, at its core it is as phony as those underwater "boulders" at Disney World that turn out, upon close inspection, to have been manufactured from a material bearing a suspicious resemblance to Styrofoam.

To be sure, precisely for this reason there is something quite apt in the selection of Williamsburg as the spot at which to treat the high panjandri of the civilized world to an orgy of Americana. Given the choice between the ersatz and the authentic, Americans will zero in on the former with unerring accuracy. In a country where image carries greater weight than actuality, where the recital of ingredients on a can of soup reads as if it were a shopping list for the military-industrial complex, where the highest elected official took his intellectual apprenticeship in the celluloid land of make-believe—in such a country, Colonial Williamsburg is an all-too-accurate embodiment of the national ethos.

Williamsburg is not, as it is represented to be, the past; it is a reconstruction of the past as we wish it to have been, complete with all modern conveniences. If only Mickey and Minnie were there, prancing down the stairs of the governor's palace and crooning "It's a Small World," Williamsburg would embrace within its tidy boundaries just about everything that simultaneously exploits and debases our hard, painful history. For the benefit of the contemporary visitor, whether he be a Socialist French president or a reactionary American president, Williamsburg presents an Olde America that has been sanitized beyond recognition.

In a word, Williamsburg is *cute*—in just the same artificial, cloying, idealized way that the town square in Disney World is *cute.* It's so darn cute 'n' quaint that you just want to hug everyone and everything you see: the mechanically dulcet-voiced women in their Colonial frocks and bonnets who hustle you along from one attraction to another; the sturdy laborers and craftsmen in their breeches and aprons who make merry tunes on the smithy's anvil; the immaculate little houses snuggled up in their adorable rows; the majestic capitol with its spit 'n' polish fixtures and its guides in gleaming livery and powdered wigs. It's all so, well, *historic* that it just makes you proud to be an American.

It's called a "historic preservation area," which is a joke. Williamsburg is actually a theme park, the theme being that Olde America was as pretty and as peaceable as a picture on a postcard. Williamsburg is engaged not in preserving and restoring but in prettifying and mythologizing. No sewage or human waste befouls its water, though most surely both did two and a half centuries ago in the Williamsburg we now "preserve;" no disease or epidemic darkens its air, though these were constant terrors of eighteenth-century life; no hint of crippling injury or premature death discolors the bright countenances of the costumed "residents," though these, too, were constants.

The trouble with Williamsburg is not that it lacks nitty-gritty authenticity to the nth degree—presumably not even the most literal-minded preservationist would subject the poor tourist to sewage in the gutters—but that it represents its idyllic townscape as the living past; one of its more hyperbolic publications describes it as "no dusty museum of the dead past, but rather a vividly re-created community, flourishing and alive," and that is the company line. Yes, Williamsburg is a pretty place to visit and the food in its restaurants is, at its best, very good indeed; but it's an America the Beautiful theme park, not an eighteenth-century town. It presents only an illusion of historical truth, which is to say that it encourages us—and we are most eager to be encouraged—to believe in a falsified, sanitized, sentimentalized past.

This preference for image over reality is so central to Williamsburg in its twentieth-century incarnation that it can even be said to explain the very existence of the "historic preservation area." The nonprofit foundation that has underwritten its reconstruction was set up in 1926 by John D. Rockefeller, Jr., whose life's work was image making—persuading the public that the name Rockefeller was a synonym for philanthropy instead of avarice, as personified by his notorious father. In the minds of many of his admirers, Williamsburg remains John Jr.'s finest accomplishment; that it has been a singularly successful investment in sound public relations is indisputable, since there could be no better PR than indelibly identifying the family with theme-park patriotism.

Williamsburg is also, this being America, good business. John Jr.'s foundation may be nonprofit, but daily activity in what is reverently called the Historic Area is devoted primarily to separating the tourist from his cash. The real center of Colonial Williamsburg is not the capitol, where the House of Burgesses sat; it's the Craft House, where some of the priciest goods this side of Tiffany's are marketed in wholesale lots. Going to Williamsburg is like going to New York; every time you turn around there's someone's hand in your pocketbook, though in

Williamsburg the hand is at least soft and agreeably scented.

One of the articles for sale at Craft House the last time I was there was a book by Carl Bridenbaugh called *Jamestown: 1544–1699*, a history of the brief life of the older settlement a few miles away on the James River. Maybe no one on the store's staff had read it, because so far as the image of early America fostered by Colonial Williamsburg is concerned, this is a subversive document. In heartbreaking detail, it describes the struggle to settle Virginia: the filthy, perilous and pestilential conditions of daily life; the bitter animosity between the powerful few and the debased many; the control of government by an assembly that was neither democratic nor popular; the gruesome ways in which early settlers came to their early deaths. It is "a somber chronicle, one unrelieved by either merriment or an attitude of warm humanity."

The drive from Williamsburg to Jamestown is short, but the agenda indicates that Ronald Reagan and the other luminaries will not be making it. This, when you think about it, is not surprising. Jamestown, in its permanent state of excavation, is the real thing: a tiny spot, desolate but beautiful, the foundations of its mean houses huddled together against the Indians and the weather and the unknown—the place where America began. Williamsburg, by contrast, is a period piece that has been constructed to suit the convenience and self-interest of hindsight. It is the way we want to see ourselves, so it stands to reason that it is also the way we present ourselves to the world.

Letting It All Hang Out

August 29, 1983

In this age of unfettered "liberation"—of unrestrained self-adoration and self-absorption—"honesty" above all is said to be the best policy, reticence the worst. The heroes of the age are those who march before the cameras, whether they be Phil Donahue's or Dan Rather's or Jane Pauley's, and invite the world to "share" their secrets. On the path to "self-fulfillment," confession is the first and most important order of business.

Thus we have the congressional odd couple of the summer of 1983, Robert Bauman and Gerry Studds. The former, having spent a couple of years trying to justify his involvement in men's room solicitation on the grounds that booze mixed up with "homosexual tendencies" made him do it, suddenly leaped out of the closet and proclaimed not merely his homosexuality but his determination to devote his allegedly legendary political and organizational skills to the homosexual cause. Going public, Bauman told any interviewer within whispering distance, made him feel very good.

At about the same time, Studds was acknowledging the validity of charges that he had once had a sexual relationship with a male congressional page. In the course of this acknowledgment he not merely confessed but declared his homosexuality, after which he said he felt "great." This prompted Dana Hornig, a sympathetic journalist from Studd's district in Massachusetts, to write an article that eventually found its way into Washington's *City Paper*. Of Studds's "coming out" Hornig had this to say:

"What has come out as well, at least for the moment, is great relief. Gerry Studds today, for the first time since the Tenth District became acquainted with him, can truly be himself. In fact, today he is soaring with a new sense of liberation. He feels wonderful. He feels exhilarated. He feels strong."

That paragraph provides a succinct (and suitably sappy) summary of the new orthodoxy: Keeping one's intimate tastes and proclivities to oneself is bad, trotting them out for public examination is good; the unrevealed person is private and thus mysterious, which is bad, while the person who declares all "can truly be himself," which is good; exercising restraint in the expression of one's "feelings" is bad, letting them go for all the world to see is good. The operative assumption is that the more a person confesses, the more "known" and "liberated" he becomes.

Not merely is this the new orthodoxy; it is the new sentimentality. Without it, Phil and Merv and all the other blow-dried sob sisters of videoland would go out of business, because confession brings a tear to the eye and thus keeps the viewer hooked. For a man to give public notice of his preference for boys over girls is regarded not as a gratuitous invasion of the privacy of others but as an act of "courage" in which all of us, as fellow citizens in the land of holistic hugging, are obliged to participate as rapt observers. Indeed, our witness is not enough; our applause is expected as well, and if we fail to deliver it we stand guilty of insufficient empathy.

Which is to say that we fail to distinguish between private anguish and public display; we believe that without the latter, the former cannot really exist. It is not enough now for a homosexual to undergo the process of self-examination—by all accounts a brutally painful one—that results in his private acknowledgment of his sexual nature; it is now necessary to "come out," rather in the fashion of a young woman of station making her way into the ballrooms of society. We seem to think it insufficient for a homosexual to break the news to family and friends; telegrams must be sent to Phil and Merv, and the gossip columnists, and the editors of *Time* and *Newsweek.*

In this distasteful process, what is most distasteful: the public's insatiable thirst for gossip or false intimacy, or the individual's longing for display, for absolution by publicity? It's a toss-up. The elaborate rationales by which it is argued that self-display is good for you doubtless have far less to do with society's desire that individuals be helped in conquering their difficulties than with a yearning to legitimize prurience. If it is good for people to let it all hang out, then it is equally good for us to listen to what we want to hear: the most intimate details of the private lives of others, details that at once satisfy our longing for titillation and give us a sense of superiority—in particular moral superiority—to those who confess them.

But the urge for display is no prettier. Confession, no matter how difficult it may initially be, is in certain respects simply another way of being the center of attention. Listening to the more vociferous homosexual-rights pressure groups, it is easy to be convinced that they are less concerned with dragging people out of closets than they are with forcing themselves into the public eye. In this respect, "coming out" is not liberation but exhibitionism—yet another variation on the Me Decade's narcissistic demands for notice, approval and self-celebration.

In the cases of Bauman and Studds, to be sure, the primary impetus for "coming out" was involuntary: One was in trouble with the law and the other with his colleagues, and both for reasons connected to homosexuality. But having been forced out into the open, both gentlemen seem to have decided to go the full confessional route. It is difficult for people of the political persuasion to resist the eye of the camera, no matter why it is directed at them, and both of these highly political fellows seem to have gotten the desire to cleanse their linen in public all mixed up with a no less powerful desire to recover, by means of the sympathy factor, as much lost political ground as possible.

Well, it is possible to sympathize with anyone who finds

himself in a painful fix—whether having to do with sex, or illness, or marital discord, or behavioral eccentricity, or what have you—and still to find it repugnant that he insists on "sharing" these intimacies with the entire family of man. Perhaps, in an age that takes its pieties and profundities from Leo Buscaglia and Rod McKuen and Jane Fonda, this is "honesty." But viewed without the tinted glasses of pop psychology it can be seen for what it really is: mere self-indulgence, made all the more distasteful by the complacently arrogant assumption that one is interesting or important enough to force oneself upon the attention of people to whom one has never been introduced.

The "Higher" Education

December 19, 1983

A college in New Jersey got itself a few inches of newspaper space last week by sending forth the news that in the spring of the new year it will offer, under the auspices of a professor of anthropology, three courses built around the television program *M*A*S*H*. The professor explained that his hope is thereby to lure students into the study of history, drama, and sociology:

"The idea was inspired by the response of my students to the last episode of *M*A*S*H*. It was one of the few events that got students interested and involved in the past few years. . . . More and more, students look at college as vocational and technical school. They are taking courses of immediate impact. In that kind of atmosphere, we can't expect our students to be ready and eager to get involved in the classics."

Could there be a more succinct statement of the doleful condition of what now passes for "higher" education in much of the United States? It is difficult to imagine one. In a mere five sentences, this well-intentioned member of the professoriat managed, however inadvertently, to cover these phenomena: the indifference of the pampered children of the American middle class to anything remotely approximating culture, not to mention serious thought; the passive acceptance by this generation of collegians of anything handed along to it by way of the television screen; the assumption, by this generation as by much of the nation, that television reality is actual reality; the continuing degeneration of American colleges and universities into trade schools, not to mention baby-sitters for idle late adolescents; and the willingness, indeed the fawning eagerness, of the education establishment to lower its standards in order to keep these children enrolled and thus keep itself in business.

It is this last matter that is most discouraging of all. To be sure, colleges have always offered a handful of courses designed to give students a break or to ease the passage of athletes and other mercenaries: Philosophy of Recreation 101, Principles of Child-Rearing 202, and needless to say the legendary Basket Weaving 303—even at Stanford or Yale, the student in desperate need of a crip course can be sure to find one. By the same token, there have always been professors with soft grading standards, lax attendance requirements, casual attitudes toward classroom behavior; college isn't supposed to be easy but neither is it meant to be an unremitting grind, and the best educators as well as the worst have always recognized this.

But to organize a course around a situation comedy and to represent it as history, drama or sociology is something else altogether. At the most obvious level it is pure if unwitting farce, the equivalent of watching *Gandhi* at the movies and then declaring oneself an expert on all matters Indian. But at a deeper and more damaging level, it is supine capitulation on the part of "higher" education to the laziness and complacency of the children whom it is ostensibly instructing; it is yet another little step along the road down which too many American colleges and universities are traveling, a road at the end of which is "education" that provides no real education at all.

To offer a course built around *M*A*S*H* and to fob it off as history or drama, even as sociology, is to turn an institution of "higher" education into a fool's paradise. It happens all the time. Students who can't or won't read Donne and Marvell and Frost are offered, instead, Rod McKuen; students who haven't the patience or interest for Fielding and Dostoyevsky and Melville are offered, instead, courses in mysteries and science fiction. The rationale, now being echoed by the professor of *M*A*S*H*, is that if we can only get them into the classroom with something they know and understand—something right out of their very own little lives—then in good time they will be seduced into better and more difficult things, grown-up things.

It's the same rationale that led people to say, when I was young, that it was okay for kids to read Classic Comics because in good time that would lead them to read classic books. But it was my experience, and that of my friends, that reading Classic Comics simply led us to read more Classic Comics. They were the painless way out. You could read the Classic Comics version of *Pride and Prejudice* and persuade yourself that you had actually read *Pride and Prejudice* itself, and therefore were well along the way to being an educated person, which in fact you would be just as soon as you had read the Classic Comics version of *Don Quixote*, which was of course a much tougher Classic Comic.

Teaching a "history" course in *M*A*S*H* or a "poetry" course in Rod McKuen and calling it part of a college education is the equivalent of letting kids read Classic Comics and certifying them as steeped in the riches of literature. It's a cop-out and a fraud: a cop-out because it allows both the student and the teacher to evade the hard business of learning, a fraud because in the end what it leads to is a college degree and its explicit statement that the person who holds it is educated.

This degree may indeed legitimately assert that the person holding it is educated to operate a computer, supervise an engineering project or practice accountancy; these are important skills, and obtaining a sophisticated education in their use is an absolutely valid reason for attending an institution that offers advanced training. But the ability to operate a computer is one thing and a decent knowledge of the world's history is quite another; if an institution is really in the business of offering the former and can only maintain a pretense of the latter, it ought to abandon that pretense forthwith and acknowledge that it is a trade school rather than a college. To do otherwise is to lie—to its students, to itself, to society—about the nature of the "education" that can be obtained there.

*M*A*S*H* was a dandy television show, as television shows

go, but that is all it ever was; it had about as much to do with the actual history of the Korean War as military music has to do with music. For an institution of "higher" learning to suggest to its students that this television show was "history" is a cruel deception, one that will encourage them in what they already want to believe: that there are easy answers to the hard questions of life. But such deception is the order of the day; soon enough, as a predictable consequence, we will be a nation of Valley Girls.

“Projecting” the News

March 5, 1984

People who worry about the unpleasant odor currently clinging to the press will do well to give more than passing consideration to the minor controversy over “vote projections” on television news broadcasts. Though this does not seem to be a matter over which the public at large has become unduly exercised, it provides an especially revealing illustration of why the press is so widely regarded with suspicion and distaste.

Vote projections are those technological toys that have taken all the fun out of election night. In the good old days—and, hey, listen, they *were* good—people huddled around the radio or television set for hours as the returns trickled in from hill country Texas and downstate Illinois. The only way to determine the outcome of elections was, oddly enough, to count the votes; it was often a hard day's night before they were all in, but the suspense and camaraderie more than compensated for the long wait.

Now, thanks to entrance polls and exit polls and computerized analyses of voting patterns, we know what we've done before we've done it. Right around dinnertime here comes Dan Rather, throbbing like a teenager in terminal heat, screeching that with 1 percent of the votes counted in Aroostook County, CBS News has projected that Maine will give 53 percent of its votes to Ronald McDonald. Since the nation goes as Maine goes, we can all turn the dial to reruns of *Gilligan's Island*. Fun's over, folks.

But fun unfortunately is not the issue here. Among politicians, there is widespread and genuine concern that the premature projection of winners and losers may discourage people from voting in areas where the polls are still open. Among members of the press, there should be—though apparently there is not—equally widespread and genuine concern that these projections are classic examples of the arrogant, self-serving behavior that has turned so many Americans, with ample reason, against those of us who bring the news.

It is the contention of various spokesmen for the networks specifically and the news business generally that any restriction on the reporting of vote projections would be an infringement of First Amendment "rights." The pertinent words in that amendment read as follows: "Congress shall make no law . . . abridging the freedom of speech, or of the press. . . ." Nowhere in those words, no matter how liberally or imaginatively they are read, is there the slightest suggestion that these freedoms include a "right" to equate vote projections with actual election returns and to broadcast (or publish) them as such.

Yet this is precisely what the networks do. The various caveats offered by the breathless anchormen and breathless reporters—"Now, remember, these are only projections!" "Get out and vote, America!"—are nothing except smokescreens. The networks know that in all but a handful of cases the projections will hold up, and they know that we know it. They deal out just enough cautionary mumbo jumbo to placate their critics on Capitol Hill, and then they put the numbers on the screen.

One of those critics is Timothy Wirth, a congressman from Colorado who has taken a particular interest in mass communications. After the New Hampshire primary he said that he thought the networks "were all very careful to qualify their estimates" in reporting the results, which actually seems true only in comparison with their unseemly haste the previous week in reporting on the Iowa primary; to all intents and purposes, after all, they gave New Hampshire to Gary Hart before the cocktail hour was over, which isn't exactly blushing reticence.

Wirth said that the matter is not susceptible to congressional resolution ("You can't legislate good judgment") and then made an important point: "The issue is what public good is achieved by early predictions and how that balances off against the harm when early predictions discourage voters." This is the question that gives the networks difficulty, no doubt because they know full well that the "public good" is just about the last thing on their minds when they send forth these projections.

There's plenty of talk, to be sure, from network mouthpieces and others about "the public's right to know," as if this somehow were sufficient justification for announcing news before it has actually happened. But that's merely another smokescreen. What the talk is really about is the "right" of the network news organizations to compete with each other; these projections have nothing to do with serious reporting and everything to do with each news organization's desire to put points on the board against the others.

In the hermetic, macho world of television news, competition is the name of the game: competition for ratings points and audience shares, competition for "prestige," competition for the bragging rights to P. J. Clarke's and the Italian Pavilion. Such is the capacity of the human mind for folly that being first by thirty-three seconds with a vote projection can become crucial to "winning" this competition and thus enjoying the heady thrills of triumph. Make no mistake about it: Being first is the purpose of the vote projections. The "public good," the "public's right to know," the "public interest"—these lofty considerations have nothing at all to do with the networks' reasons for airing them.

So what we have here is a clear-cut example of the bizarre assumption that the medium delivering the news is of greater consequence than the news itself. The vote projections exist not to inform us out there in the audience but to inflate the institutional egos of the network news organizations—to prove that CBS is faster than NBC, that ABC has better graphics than CBS, that NBC has more skillfull pollsters than ABC. It is a "philosophy" of journalism the essence of which is: Watch what we do, not what we report.

This narcissistic view, which is by no means limited to television news, has much to do with the public's hostility to and distrust of the press. What it says to the public is: You don't matter, *we* matter; your votes don't count, *our* votes count. The vote projections masquerade as news, but they're really just another way for the press to tell itself how wonderful and how important it is. Small wonder the public feels otherwise.

Art Critics on the Dole

April 9, 1984

The notion that the federal government has an obligation to give financial support to art critics is most kindly described as peculiar, but it does have its supporters. Many of them, you will not be surprised to learn, are art critics. Now many art critics are up in arms because the government has had second thoughts about giving them grants, and accordingly has suspended a fellowship program it has operated for a dozen years.

The suspension has been ordered by Frank Hodsoll, chairman of the National Endowment for the Arts, which since 1972 has given more than $650,000 to some 180 critics of the visual arts. His action is the latest round in a controversy over the value of the fellowships, which originally were designed to encourage and improve art criticism—a dubious task for the government if ever there was one—and which have been given in amounts from $1,000 to $10,000, with the average being a little over $3,600. The suspension, according to Hodsoll, is intended to give the endowment time to review the program in order to determine its effectiveness.

The reaction of those art critics who spoke last week with a reporter for the *New York Times* was predictably negative. "We're very disappointed," one said. "Many of us feel that American art criticism is a bit of a disaster area, with regard to the lowly state of the critic—particularly economic—and also its general intellectual poverty. The endowment shouldn't walk away, but should attempt to raise the level of criticism and better the lot of art critics." Another said: "When this decision is finally understood, it will embitter the visual arts community. . . . This is the first time the bureaucracy in Washington has acted in direct opposition to one of the major constituencies it is supposed to serve and encourage."

The notion of art critics as a "major constituency" is almost as hilarious as the notion of book reviewers as a "major" constituency, but let it pass. The point is that these gentlemen—and others, apparently, in the community of the visual arts—have somehow managed to persuade themselves that the government of the United States owes them and their fellow critics a living. What they seem to have in mind is a form of welfare for the intellectually deserving; if you can't make a living out there in the real world writing about art, then it's the government's obligation to come to your aid because—this seems to be the underlying assumption—the writing you do is necessary to the evolution of a fully rounded society.

The assumption is utterly without foundation. Only a fully rounded art critic stands to benefit from government subsidies for art critics. Society has no more discernible interest in funding the flowering of a thousand art critics than it does in subsidizing the instruction of place kickers or head waiters. If the private economy does not support art critics in the style to which they would like to become accustomed, the taxpayers certainly have no obligation to do so. It may or may not be unfortunate, depending on one's point of view, that society has turned so deaf an ear to the needs of its art critics; but it is a bizarre twist of logic to argue that since the private economy has only marginal interest in art criticism, the public treasury—which of course is supported by the private economy—should keep it afloat.

Quite apart from the basic point that no entitlement exists, there is the question of how effectively the National Endowment program has managed to serve its original purpose. The clear suggestion of a sympathetic and knowledgeable observer is that it has not. John Beardsley, an authority on art, was asked a year ago by the endowment to make a report on the program's progress. Beardsley is a believer in the idea of "financial or moral support for critics," and his objective was "to strengthen the program, not to defeat it." Nevertheless, his report was hardly encouraging to the program's apologists.

With what gives every indication of being wry understatement, Beardsley observed that the fellowships "provide a psychological and financial boost to their recipients." Beyond that, though, "there is little evidence that they positively affect the character and quality of the recipients' work, and even less that they help to raise the standards of art criticism more generally." He also noted—this being a criticism frequently directed at N.E.A. during its salad days in the 1970s—that there was evidence of "specific ideological biases" at work in the process by which fellowship recipients were chosen; or, to put it another way, bedfellows were known to provide for bedfellows.

This would seem ample justification for tossing the critics' welfare fund into the scrap heap where many far more valuable programs have landed in these Reagan years, but it has hardly persuaded the art critics. A number of them argue, in a letter to Hodsoll, that "the grants were important because criticism is important"—a highly debatable assumption in the first place and a line of reasoning that any amateur logician could rip to shreds in the second. By the same reasoning, the federal government should offer fellowships to promote the lost craft of bunting, since in our great national pastime of baseball bunting is very important indeed—perhaps even more important than art criticism.

The fear among art critics is that the "suspension" is merely a bit of going through the motions on Hodsoll's part—that it is really the prelude to killing the program altogether. Only he can say whether this is what he has in mind, and at the moment all he is saying is that "we are committed to exploring potential solutions seriously," which, to be sure, is the sort of thing people in politically sensitive positions are given to saying just before the axe falls.

But if the axe is what is in store, it will be bad news only for that very small number of people for whom the program has been a source of found money. Just about everyone else can only regard it as an enterprise richly deserving one of Senator William Proxmire's awards for preposterous government spending. The federal government has no more business handing out individual grants to art critics, or music critics, or theater critics, or restaurant critics, or book critics—than it has telling writers what to write or musicians what to play. This little boondoggle may have been a good thing for a handful of art critics, but it's been a rip-off of the taxpayer. Where's your hatchet, Hodsoll?

"I'm a Legitimate Class"

June 18, 1984

The 1920s, American mythology has had it for a half century, were the "Golden Age of Sport." You know: Babe Ruth, Bill Tilden, Bobby Jones, Red Grange—heroes who even now seem larger than life, and certainly a whole lot larger than most of the Dollar Bills who dominate sport today. But heroes notwithstanding, American mythology has it wrong: the Golden Age of Sport isn't the twenties but the eighties, because it's during the eighties that sport has at last entered the temple of respectability.

Yes, you guessed it: In the 1980s sport has become a subject of academic inquiry and instruction. In this enlightened decade it is now, after all these years, possible to study sport in college just the way it is possible to study *M*A*S*H* and the movies of Alfred Hitchcock and other subjects of transcendent scholarly importance. Sport has become an academic discipline all its own, just like English and history and comparative literature.

It's gotten so respectable in scholarly circles, in fact, that it even has its own professional academic association. Just as the drones of the English departments have their Modern Language Association and those of the history departments their American Historical Association, so the pedants of sport have the North American Society for Sport History. This august body held its twelfth annual convention in Louisville last week, an occasion about which the Associated Press reported: "In recent years, the convention has become a celebration as greater recognition is given the field, educators say."

Educators. Let's put that in italics, just to emphasize the dignity and stature of it all. *Educators*. And what do they teach? Well, Gene Murdock of Marietta College in Ohio has a course called "Sports and American Life," which considers among other weighty matters "things like how the industrial age affected sports equipment," the professor says. At the University of Massachusetts you can study, if that's the word for it, women and sport history as taught by Betty Spears, who is a pathfinder: "Most of our theses haven't been tested before," she says, "so we have to pave the way instead of expanding on what other people think," which if nothing else makes her a considerable rarity on today's academic scene.

The incoming president of the society, J. Thomas Jable, who teaches physical education at William Paterson College of New Jersey, speaks of the great strides sport history has made. "We have textbooks, tests, homework, the same as any other class," he says, and adds: "The students come in thinking they are taking a bunny, and go out with a whole new understanding. It's a way of getting kids interested in history and sociology by using something they like to learn about. And it brings to light an important part of history that has been ignored."

Can you *believe* it? Textbooks! Tests! Homework! Just like grown-ups! For the sports historians, it's out of the outhouse and into the penthouse. In the words of David Voigt, "professor of baseball in American culture" at Albright College in Pennsylvania: "Our motto used to be the old W. C. Fields quote, 'Give them an evasive answer,' because it was easier than saying what we did. Now I'm a legitimate class and I've been accepted by my fellow liberal arts educators."

Ah yes, acceptance. Sport has entered the groves of academe, not on the playing field but in the classroom. Fully four hundred teachers of sport history are enrolled in the North American Society for Sport History, representing as many institutions of higher learning. "We used to be composed of just physical educators," one veteran member says, "but now we have historians, sociologists, geologists and anthropologists."

Why he didn't mention English professors is a mystery, because sport has become a hot ticket in the literature departments in recent years. "Sport in Literature," or variations on that theme, is to be found in the catalogues of many "universities" these days; students get to read *The Natural* and *Bang the Drum Slowly*, and then they get to talk about metaphors and similes and all that kind of stuff. The professors say they like to read about baseball and football; maybe if they like reading about baseball and football they'll be encouraged to get into the really heavy matter. Oh, you know, like maybe J. D. Salinger and Kurt Vonnegut and Erica Jong and the other giants of our golden age.

When you get right down to it, teaching about sport in history and literature is really great. It's great for the students, because they get to think deep thoughts about Reggie Jackson and Kareem Abdul-Jabbar ("The Economics of Modern Sport") or to learn about old-timers like Ty Cobb and Jim Thorpe ("Conflict and Resolution in Ancient Sport"), and in the end they even get credit for it.

But it's every bit as great for the professors, because by conning the lazy, indulgent overlords of academe into accepting sport as a subject to research and teach, they have managed to wrap fun and games in the mantle of scholarly legitimacy. Just think: instead of spending their careers doing something *serious*, they get to be paid for being fans. Instead of stewing over intercultural conflict in suburban Los Angeles in 1953, the sociologist of sport gets to analyze shifting patterns of fan loyalty in Oakland in 1972; instead of researching mimetic devices in the early verse of John Leister Warren de Tabley, the professor of sports literature gets to collate the fugitive journalism of George Plimpton.

Sure beats working for a living, doesn't it? In fact, it's just about the best life a fellow could ask for. On the one hand he gets to spend his days going to ball games (primary research) and reading the sports pages (secondary research) and even, if he gets incredibly lucky, talking with real, live athletes (oral-history research). Yet on the other hand he gets to be a full-fledged member of the academic club ("I'm a legitimate class and I've been accepted by my fellow liberal-arts educators"), which means all manner of nice things: tenure, membership in the faculty club, a couple of hours a week in the office, the right to be called "Professor."

And then when he gets together once a year with his fellow scholars, what does he get to do? Well, a convention is a convention, so he's got to sit around and listen to scholarly papers: heavy stuff, like urbanization and professional sports, sports and war in ancient times, sports and organizations in modern society. Ho, hum. But that doesn't take long, and then the fun begins: a minor league baseball game between Louisville and Indianapolis, a tour of the Churchill Downs race track, another tour of the Hillerich & Bradley baseball bat factory. Onward and upward with scholarship!

Selling Out

February 25, 1985

In the land of the free and the home of the brave, these developments took place last week:

• Auditions began in New York for a Broadway musical called *Mayor.* It is written by Warren Leight, with songs by Charles Strouse, and is budgeted at $228,000. It is based on the book of the same title by Edward I. Koch, the city's mayor.

• Geraldine Ferraro's participation in a television commercial for Diet Pepsi was predicted by *Advertising Age* and confirmed by the *Washington Post.* Ferraro, who was the Democratic nominee for the vice presidency last year, will be paid more than $500,000 for the commercial, in which she is shown chatting with her two daughters and advising them that "there are lots of choices for women and one of the choices is that you can be a mother," the precise pertinence of which to Diet Pepsi presumably will be revealed at some future date.

• Ralph Nader sent a letter to President Reagan urging him, as "custodian of matters relating to presidential taste and decorum," to "urge that businesses rein in their promotional addictions and permit the historical record, not advertising sleaze, to speak for our past presidents and founders." Nader's ample supply of indignation was in this instance set off by television commercials depicting the likes of Thomas Jefferson, Benjamin Franklin, George Washington and Abraham Lincoln peddling everything from banks to (Japanese!) automobiles.

Not for the first time, Nader thereby put on public display his bottomless capacity for naïveté. Surely he cannot imagine that a man who came to the White House by way of fronting for General Electric is going to be offended at the sight of presidents leaving the White House and fronting for other enterprises—even if those presidents are many generations dead and are portrayed in these commercials by actors, for whom as a breed, as it happens, the incumbent has deep affection. Surely, by the same token, Nader cannot imagine that anybody, in this age of sleaze, is going to be offended by yet another exploitation of public position for private gain.

The surprise isn't that Tommy Jefferson is hustling banks but that Ralph Nader is surprised. The ad agency that came up with the idea of using George Washington—"Nutty George," as Bob Newhart used to call him—to push Nissan automobiles was just playing by the rules of the game, as the game is now played. In the United States of Glitz, the ultimate mark of prestige is not election to high public office but the opportunity to prostitute one's dignity and integrity—if, that is, one ever had any of either—in a television commercial. In going show biz the politicians, both dead and alive, are merely doing what politicians always do: following the crowd.

What did Sam Ervin do after lecturing the nation, month upon month, about momentous matters of ethics and morality? He signed himself up as a shill for American Express. What did Gerald Ford do after two years of healing our national wounds? He signed up for those two indistinguishable, interchangeable American institutions, the celebrity golf tour and the college lecture circuit. What do all White House custodians, United States senators and Foreign Service plenipotentiaries do the moment the opportunity presents itself? They write books, or, with the aid of ghosts, they "author" them.

Public service isn't public service anymore, if ever it was. It's the springboard to Fat City, the land of grasp and grab, where sly fellows turn the notoriety acquired through public office into the real coin of the realm, plugola. Edward Koch may

 have assumed office with every intention of being the best mayor since Abraham Beame, but it didn't take him long to grind out a book—the most unlikely best seller of recent vintage—and then to suggest that it would make a dandy Broadway show; Geraldine Ferraro may have accepted her nomination with every hope of speaking for newly liberated woman, but when Bantam Books ($1 million) and Diet Pepsi ($500,000) came courting, she was as willing as a Southern belle being romanced by Rhett Butler.

Money, money, money: Can you use any money today? That's the question Ethel Merman asked in *Call Me Madam*, and it's the question to which the guys and dolls of politics respond with a thundering chorus of "Gimme!" Never in our history has the line between grasping for political power and grasping for personal riches been more difficult to distinguish. A presidential adviser writes a diet book while in office, and no one seems offended by what gives every appearance of being an effort to capitalize on the prominence of his public position; no one seems to be offended because no one *is* offended in a capital city where such exploitation has become a fact of daily life.

Where's Ralph Nader been all this time, anyway? As usual, the guy simply is out to lunch. Instead of saving the world, he ought to be strip-mining it. He's got a *name*, and it's a cinch the fellows in ad alley would say he's got *credibility*. Surely there's a spot for Ralph in the Miller Lite gang, maybe filling in for Rodney Dangerfield or Bob Uecker from time to time. Don't you know Lee Iacocca would love to get his hands on Ralph? "Hello there. I'm Ralph Nader. When I go out for a day of raiding, I go in my Chrysler. I wouldn't drive anything else. It's got seat belts, air bags and a registered nurse in the trunk. It's safe at (wink!) *any* speed!"

Run that through the Super Bowl a few times and before you can say "Ed McMahon" Ralph Nader would be famous. Not Jack Kemp famous, or Bob Dole famous, or Cap Weinberger famous, but *famous.* You know: Dinah Shore famous, Chuck Yeager famous, Robert Young famous. And soon to be Gerry Ferraro famous. Soon the kids will be saying about her, "I didn't know the Diet Pepsi lady ran for vice president," just the way they already say, "I didn't know Mr. Coffee used to play baseball."

It's the new American immortality, and Nader is just whistling Dixie if he thinks anyone in Washington, dead or alive, is going to say no when it beckons. "Howdy! I'm Honest Abe! You'll find the cheapest deals in town under the sign of the stovepipe hat! Seventy-nine Malibu, four on the floor, make me an offer! I don't split rails, I split the difference! Got an eighty-two Mustang that's screamin' to leave the lot! It's got YOU written all over it! At Honest Abe's, no offer is too low and the customer is king! Come on out to Honest Abe's and I'll give you a T-shirt just for takin' a test drive! I'm Honest Abe, and I ain't got NO malice toward noooooooooooBODY!"

Hick Chic

March 25, 1985

Here's a tip for trendies: Keep an eye out for Hick Chic. The first to spot it was my friend the ferociously opinionated novelist, who recently sent along this order: "Here is your assignment. Would you please write an essay explaining why in a nation full of yuppies, conservatives and materialists, with college campuses full of business students and future lawyers, rural poverty is all the rage, as in *Love Medicine* and *The Beans of Egypt, Maine*?"

The books to which she refers are, respectively, a collection of interconnected short stories by Louise Erdrich about poor rural Indians in South Dakota and a novel by Carolyn Chute about poor rural white folks in Maine. They are indeed all the rage. *Love Medicine* has won the National Book Critics Circle's prize for fiction, and *The Beans of Egypt, Maine* has actually managed to work its way onto the lower rungs of the paperback best-seller lists.

If these books were isolated phenomena they could be dismissed as such, but they are not. Ever in search of fads to embrace, the urban middle class has descended on the boondocks with a vengeance. New Yorkers, in their pricey punk raiment, crowd into with-it restaurants that feature the cookery of rural Louisiana (Cajun) or Texas (Tex-Mex) or North Carolina (Bar-B-Que). What used to be called hillbilly music has in recent years put on glitzy airs, renamed itself "country," and offered up a sanitized sound that urbanites, in their infinite ignorance of all things alien, fancy to be the real thing.

Hick is big in the movies, too, especially if it involves beleaguered farmers desperately clinging to their own postage stamps of native soil. Jessica Lange and Sam Shepard are the Ma and Pa Kettle of the eighties, Sally Field bids fair to be the reincarnation of Ma Joad, and Jane Fonda out-minnies Minnie Pearl. From *Country* to *Witness* to *Places in the Heart*, Hollywood's gone so consarned bucolic it jes' about makes you want to snap your galluses and fiddle up a few rounds of "Turkey in the Straw."

Not merely that, but surely as night follows day the academics follow the trendies, and so it is that "a new rural history" is sweeping through the campuses. According to a report last week in the *Chronicle of Higher Education,* there is now "a 'rural history network' within the Social Science History Association 'to stimulate and discuss the new history' " that members of the profession are now unearthing. All of this mighty labor has borne fruit, and our knowledge is being expanded through documents bearing such titles as *German Seed in Texas Soil: Immigrant Farmers in Nineteenth-Century Texas* and (this sounds especially appealing) *Frontier Farming in an Urban Shadow: The Influence of Madison's Proximity on the Agricultural Development of Blooming Grove, Wisconsin.*

That the academics are on the prowl amid the silos and haystacks is easy enough to explain: The academics are *always* on the prowl, especially of late in the history departments, where the current fashion for "grass-roots history" has rendered virtually anything a respectable subject for study. If we're going to have "grass-roots history," then what could be better than to study, well, the grass and the roots? Plow on!

But the explosion of Hick Chic among the urbanites and the yuppies is, as my perplexed friend suggests, rather more difficult to fathom. The only green objects of which these people have any direct experience are ferns, the only red-dirt ones are exposed bricks, and the only harvests that really meaning anything to them are the ones in Colombia. The fad scarcely seems explained by an atavistic longing for the land, since these people

 are entirely too shallow to have longings any deeper than those for Bavarian automobiles, French chocolates and Swiss holidays.

But therein may lie the explanation, or at least an explanation. The urban faddists haven't fastened on Hick Chic out of any inherent merit or interest that they discern in it, but because they see it as yet another product with which to bedeck their lives. The real life of the countryside is as distant to them as the real life of Jupiter, perhaps even more so, and even if it was right at hand it would hold no appeal for them. What they like is the *idea* of country and the various artifacts associated with it.

The idea of country is that there are all these really earthy people out there in places like Arkansas and Georgia—you know, people like Sally Field and Jane Fonda—who do all these quaint things with the land, just the way the transplanted yuppies do in Vermont. Yes, they lead a hard life (thank God it's them and not us), but there's a nobility of soul to their daily labors that sends a shiver down the spine and a tear down the cheek, especially when the closest we ever get to it is the neighborhood art-film theater. The thing about country is that, well, gosh darn it, it makes you feel good all over. And if you're talking Amish country, that just plain makes you feel downright noble.

Especially when you're surrounded by the artifacts of country—artifacts, as has now been amply documented, being what urban trendy is really all about. Going country means that you get to order all these neat things from all those neat catalogues that are every good yuppie's leisure reading matter. You get to order Shaker furniture—you can even make it yourself, from kits, if you go for the hands-on approach to self-gratification—and quilts made up from the cutest old odds and ends of cloth. When it's time to water your ferns you can put on your dungarees—not bluejeans, mind you, but real country dungarees—and if you want to, you can close your eyes and pretend you're sloppin' the hawgs, just the way Buddy Ebsen used to do it.

But what we're talking about isn't *The Beverly Hillbillies*, not for a moment. That witless old television show was strictly for proles, for the great unwashed—for country people, if you will. No, what we're talking about now is country for the new sophisticates, the people who know that the ultimate destiny of barns is to be rehabbed into nouvelle cuisine restaurants. After all these years of struggling, country has made it: Country is *hot.* With an oink-oink here, and an oink-oink there, here an oink, there an oink, everywhere an oink-oink! And wouldn't Jeremy Irons be wonderful as Old MacDonald?

Trapped on Campus

April 1, 1985

The times they are a-changing on the college campuses, and don't for a moment believe otherwise. Not merely is higher education subject to all the outside pressures that have been so much in the news recently, most notably the Reagan administration's proposal to reduce student-loan programs and the reports by various influential committees demanding various changes in undergraduate instruction; beyond that, America's colleges and universities are being traumatically affected by large economic and social developments that are completely beyond their control.

This came home to me with something of a jolt last week during a visit to a medium-size university in the Midwest. It is a publicly supported institution, a second-tier school in a three-tier statewide system at the top of which is the state university, in the middle regional universities, and at the bottom four-year colleges. It began its existence as a normal school, and indeed to considerable measure remains one now, since the education of prospective teachers remains its principal business. But during the higher-education explosion of the 1960s it took on the name if not the real function of a university; now, like so many comparable institutions throughout the country, it is learning the hard facts of campus life in the postsixties era.

The most pervasive of these is the end of the baby boom and the subsequent drop in enrollment. Only a few years ago this school had more than twelve thousand students on campus; now that number has fallen to around nine thousand. The school has been fortunate in that a number of faculty positions fell vacant in recent years, and its administration had the wisdom not to fill them. Thus it is not stuck with more faculty than it needs, a situation that has forced other colleges in the region into unpleasant confrontations over tenure rights. Even so, though, the enrollment decline and the subsequent revenue losses have made painfully evident that the palmy days of the sixties are ancient history, and history most unlikely to be repeated in the foreseeable future.

Another characteristic of the education boom that has disappeared is faculty mobility. If there was a recurrent theme to my conversations with teachers at this institution, it was that their individual prospects are far less bright than when they first decided to enter higher education. With the shrink in enrollment has come a brutal change in the job market. The foot soldiers of academia—the instructors, assistant professors and associate professors—no longer can expect to move upward by switching from employer to employer, as so many people do in other white-collar occupations, because there are no jobs to which they can jump. The jobs are all taken, and the people who have them are holding on for dear life.

The result is that the younger faculty members who had initially thought that their jobs at this provincial institution would merely be stepping-stones to positions at more eminent universities are now resigning themselves to the prospect of spending the rest of their careers here—and praying they will get the job security that tenure brings. This is a blessing for their employer, which finds itself with a better faculty than it might otherwise be able to attract, and for their students, who may well walk away from college with a better education than they'd originally bargained for. It is something less than a blessing, though, for the teachers themselves.

Purely by coincidence, all of those with whom I spoke were men, and at least half of them acknowledged that coming to this backwater town—for that indeed is what it is—had placed severe strains on their marriages. Their wives are smart, educated women, many of whom gave up good jobs elsewhere in order to accompany their husbands on what they, too, thought would be a brief stop on the career ladder. Now that the stop looks to be permanent, these women are shopping for work—and finding it hard to come by in a community that doesn't offer much beyond farms, stores and the university.

It's hard not to feel for these people. The end of the education boom is a good and necessary thing because matters boomed all out of proportion, but there's a human cost to the process of shrinkage, and some decent people are paying it. The teachers are lucky to have jobs, and quick to tell you how lucky they are, but there's a bitter edge to their words. Many of them are midwesterners who love their land and want to stay there, but their sights had been set on the bright lights of that region—Iowa City or Lincoln, Boulder or Columbia—rather than on a place that, in the description of a teacher at another provincial school, is "the end of the earth." One especially bright young man with whom I spoke tried mightily to be optimistic about the years that lie ahead of him, but he sounded for all the world as if he were talking not about life but about a life sentence.

People make do with the straws they draw; these teachers—and their wives—are no exceptions. Outside the classroom they organize professional associations, involve themselves in student undertakings and otherwise try to make their days as interesting as possible. Inside the classroom, though, they express frustration over the restraints that are now being placed on curricula. With evident longing they look back to the sixties and seventies, when anything really did go and teachers could teach whatever they jolly well pleased. Mystery fiction, soap operas, gay movies—you name it, the campus not merely had a place for it but would give students three credits for pretending to learn it.

All that is far from gone, alas, but the reaction against it is beginning to set in. The back-to-basics movement and the new emphasis on the core curriculum have forced some college teachers back to the nuts and bolts, and many of them are openly unhappy about it. Courses about movies and television are fun;

freshman composition courses are work. But in the new dispensation, comp is in, frills are out. This is good for colleges and good for students, and for that matter it is good for teachers, who are forced into an academic discipline that the sixties had told them they could blithely ignore.

In this instance it's difficult to feel for them; the revolution of the sixties did many terrible things to higher education in the process of doing a handful of good ones, and "innovative" courses often were among them. But even if the changes now taking place are positive and necessary, it remains that they are having hard effects on the lives of good people. To watch one's world come to pieces cannot be a happy experience, and we on the outside do well to bear that in mind even as we applaud its disappearance.

If It Hurts, Kiss It

June 10, 1985

One of the genuine oddities about the United States in the 1980s is that as it is becoming more "conservative" economically and politically, it seems to be growing more "liberal" socially and morally. There cannot be much doubt that, for the moment at least, we have repudiated the political legacy of the sixties' and seventies' activists, yet we seem to be buying their cultural legacy—of tolerance bordering on permissiveness, of openness bordering on exhibitionism—to a degree that must be startling to those who assume that political and moral conservatism go hand in hand.

Thus it is that even as we retreat from the Great Society into the Go-for-It! Society, we maintain, as many polls and some election returns indicate, surprisingly relaxed attitudes on matters of individual choice ranging from abortion to sexual preference. Indeed, those attitudes are becoming so relaxed that we may be in danger of losing our grip on ourselves, of tossing discipline and moral standards to the winds as we permit any person to do any old thing that enters his mind or his libido.

It is a climate hospitable to lunacy, as was amply demonstrated last week by the disclosure that a high school for homosexual teenagers is being financed in significant measure—about $50,000 at present—by the New York City Board of Education. Establishment of the school was proposed by something called the Institute for the Protection of Lesbian and Gay Youth, which pays the school's $500-a-month rent and contributes what the *New York Times* calls "a whole range of support services." The school is named for Harvey Milk, the homosexual San Francisco supervisor whose murder in 1978 made him something of a martyr to homosexual activists; at present the school has twenty students and meets at a church in (where else?) Greenwich Village, but its organizers hope and expect that both enrollment and physical space eventually will expand.

Ostensibly this new institution has come into being for the good of the children, who were harassed in the public schools and as a consequence dropped out. The boys in the school are described by one teacher as "overtly effeminate," the girls as "tough"; at Harvey Milk School, in what that teacher calls "an environment where gay and lesbian kids would not be subject to immature teenagers," the hope is that these students will be able to concentrate on their lessons free of hostile distractions.

What they will study is the standard curriculum with a twist, or, as one person involved with the school told the *New York Post*, "we do some things they don't do in regular high schools." That, to put it mildly, is understatement: "If we're studying poetry and Walt Whitman's name comes up, we'll point out he was gay. When we talk about history we point out that Dag Hammarskjöld was gay. Our kids have no opportunity to know the history of their people—what it means to be gay. There's more to being gay than sexuality." Another person told the *Times:* "In citizenship lessons, the teacher brings up the idea of commitment to each other, and loving and caring. In literature classes, there would be discussion of Shakespeare as a homosexual, and in history and geography the contributions gay people have made will be brought up."

The taxpayers of New York, in other words, are contributing $50,000 a year—with the prospect of larger amounts in the future—to a school that teaches a homosexually oriented interpretation of history, literature, geography and, presumably, everything else. A teacher's disclaimer to the contrary notwithstanding—"Neither in the school nor here in the institute do we convince the kids to be one way or another"—the

Harvey Milk School is clearly engaged in homosexual advocacy at, in substantial measure, public expense. Is this how New York taxpayers want their money spent?

Perhaps they do. Mayor Edward I. Koch and various school authorities apparently believe so, for there has been a chorus of official support for the school. "It is far better," according to the mayor, "to have those students in a class than wandering the streets of the city of New York and doing things that are antisocial, violative of the law or hurting themselves in some other way." According to the chancellor of the city's schools, "we have a responsibility to all youngsters to the age of twenty-one to provide them with an education. We cannot say that we are responsible for reducing dropouts and then focus our attention on only one dimension of the school population."

So what does the city do? It cooperates in the establishment of an "off-site" school designed to cater to the somewhat peculiar needs of this small group of students. It lets itself be cajoled and/or bullied by homosexual activists into cooperating in the founding of the country's first publicly supported homosexual school—which, when you get right down to it, is precisely what the Harvey Milk School is. In doing this the city not merely acknowledges, as it should, that these students have problems that demand attention; it tacitly endorses homosexuality, an endorsement that many citizens of decent, humane instincts undoubtedly will have trouble supporting.

This having been done, what is to prevent the city from funding special schools—or skating rinks, or swimming pools, or subway cars—for any other group that feels its members have been singled out for unfair treatment? To be sure, these groups may not be quite so effectively organized as homosexuals, and they may not represent voting power quite so visible or potent as the "gay vote," but in this age of "caring" and "sharing" we surely can't let their tender psyches be bruised. No, there must be an "off-site" school on every block, until at last each aggrieved pressure group is thoroughly insulated from the rest of society and allowed to be "educated" at public expense on terms most suitable to its own particular variety of grievances, preferences and/or kinks.

Some might call this caving in to special-interest pressures, but not those of us who live in the Age of Sensitivity. Our national motto is not "In God We Trust" but "If It Hurts, Kiss It," and whenever we have the chance to brighten an unhappy citizen's day, we seize it. If this means turning a school system into a conglomeration of duchies and making a mockery of the spirit and purpose of education, so be it. What matters is that everyone gets to go off and be his very own perfect self, while the rest of us stand on the sideline and applaud him for being "special."

Dirty Words

September 2, 1985

Thirty years ago the inimitable and, alas, irreplaceable Noël Coward came to the colonies with a one-man show. He took it to that citadel of urbanity, Las Vegas, where he startled the natives with a program of hilariously ribald songs. These included "A Bar on the Piccola Marina," about the unfortunate Mrs. Wentworth-Brewster's thirsty libido, and "Alice Is at It Again," about Alice who was, well, at It again, but above all there was his own rendition of Cole Porter's "Let's Do It," which contained such lines as, "Belgians and Greeks do it, / Nice young men who sell antiques do it," and "All famous writers in swarms do it, / Somerset and all the Maughams do it."

We were shocked. It was 1955; we had blushed enough already when Porter told us in *Kiss Me Kate* that "in the dark they are all the same" and when Lorenz Hart in *Pal Joey* permitted the observation by a cynical Broadway lady that "he's a laugh, but I love it, / Because the laugh's on me." These wittily risqué lyrics were very much exceptions to the rule of the day; when we sang of love three decades ago we were far more likely to ac-cen-chu-ate the positive, to sing of June and moon and spoon, than to murmur, even by indirection, of things that went on between the sheets. Small wonder Coward's lyrics seemed so daring.

So what, then, are we, who cut our eyeteeth on Georgia Gibbs and Tony Martin and Gogi Grant and Eddie Fisher, to make of the lyrics that have now aroused the indignation of the Parents Music Resource Center and the National Conference of

Parents and Teachers? How are those of us who went about sobbing "My heart cries for you, sighs for you, dies for you" going to come to grips with lyrics that deal in the most specific terms with violence, drugs, occultism and, of course, sex in all its conventional and kinky manifestations? How are we to deal even with a song so relatively tame by today's standards as Bruce Springsteen's "I'm on Fire," for singing the lyrics of which in 1955 we would have had our mouths washed out with soap?

Probably we aren't going to deal at all, for this is a whole new world. Parents and teachers are right to be angry about the scabrous lyrics to which children can now be exposed, but even if they manage to get "Parental Guidance: Explicit Lyrics" stamped on every recording by Prince or the Sex Pistols, they are most unlikely to reverse the trend. One of the saddest but most pervasive legacies of the sixties, when we let it all hang out, is that there no longer is any clear distinction between the adult and the juvenile in the murky realms of sex, profanity and worldliness. We adults may know more than the kids do, for the simple reason that we're older, but by contrast with our own youthful innocence, today's juveniles are appallingly sophisticated.

No one is to blame for any of this except ourselves. We begin in our houses, into which the general coarsening of the American language long ago crept. We use language around kids that our own parents would not have employed, even in private, between themselves, it then being quaintly thought that certain words simply did not pass between man and woman. We do not blink when, listening to children at play, we hear dirty words of four or more letters used as routinely as anything in Dick or Jane's vocabulary. The language of the streets is now the language of the rec room, and we make no particular effort to object.

Of an evening, when we sit down with the kiddies for diversions brought to us by the wits of New York and Los Angeles, we giggle together over sitcoms that leer and peek and whistle about sexual business in ways that never would have been allowed in a "sex comedy" starring Doris Day and Rock Hudson. Earlier in the day, while we were off at work or preoccupied with household chores, those same kiddies came home from school and, milk and cookies in hand, gazed their way through soap operas not much less explicit than what was once shown in movies thought to be scandalously "blue," as in *The Moon Is Blue*.

As for the omnipresent advertising to which children are subjected, much of it is predicated on the assumption that they either have active sex lives or are hard at work thinking about them. It is no exaggeration to say that the notorious Brooke Shields blue jean advertisements, at which 1980s America glances with scarcely a moment's pause, would have been centerfold material for the stag magazines of the 1950s—and would have been cause for a spanking had a nice boy been caught casting a happy eye over them. The advertising on television, all of which is seen by children, routinely makes overt sexual pitches and frequently relies on sexual jokes to get its message across.

In this climate—a climate, it must be emphasized, created entirely by adults—the lyrics of Prince and others are not so much exceptions to the norm as mild exaggerations of it. To say this is not to excuse them, but to place them in context. It is all well and good to get exercised about pop paeans to cocaine and masturbation, but to direct one's energy and anger solely toward the purveyors of pop music is rather to miss the point. We're all doing It; the only difference is that Prince is doing It a little more explicitly, a little more offensively, and very much on the public stage.

No doubt the clean-lyrics campaign now being undertaken by these parents' and teachers' groups is part of a general backlash against the new hedonism, and as such it is not unwelcome. But people need to understand that a revolution has occurred from which there is almost certainly no turning back. In the privacy of some households the old verities may still be observed, and some parents may actually bring off the admirable feat of raising their children as children rather than tiny adults, but in the society at large, "liberation" already has been accomplished.

We can't have it both ways; we can't excoriate Prince on the one hand and then snigger over *Three's Company* on the other, any more than we can deplore Madonna and then moon over *General Hospital*. The real problem isn't with rock 'n' roll but with us. Lorenz Hart wrote, "Couldn't sleep, and wouldn't sleep, / Until I could sleep where I shouldn't sleep." That's where all of us are sleeping now.

Instant Intimacy

October 28, 1985

The air is filled with the babble of intimacy. Over the telephone comes the voice of a woman to whom I have never been introduced, hoping to enlist my funds in an ostensibly charitable endeavor; "Hello, Jonathan," she begins. In the mail is a missive from a gentleman in California, previously unknown to me, seeking favors; "Dear Jonathan," he addresses me. In the doctor's office a secretary whose name I do not know hands me a sheet of paper; "Please fill out this form, Jonathan," she says.

This is the new familiarity, and there is no defense against it. In a culture whose high priests are Phil Donahue and Leo Buscaglia and Barbara Walters, to insist on a measure of formality in your dealings with persons you do not know is to mark yourself as a snob, a fuddy-duddy encrusted with the barnacles of Victorian reticence—or, as Christopher Clausen puts it in the current issue of the *American Scholar,* describing an encounter with a receptionist, as "that stuffy elitist who repelled her desire to be friendly." To address strangers by honorifics, and to expect that they in turn address you similarly, is now regarded as strictly antisocial behavior.

Our society, which likes to think of itself as "open" and "caring" and "feeling," regards this as a good thing. But Clausen does not, and neither do I. In his brief, penetrating essay "A Decent Impersonality," Clausen, who teaches English at Pennsylvania State University, argues that the trend toward "indiscriminate informality" does not enrich human relationships; it trivializes them, with unhappy consequences for both public and private life. In the former, he quite correctly notes, "it implies that personality and its expression are the only things to be valued in a public situation or servant," and "candidates for public office come more and more to be judged by the same standards as entertainers." As for private life:

"The rituals of courtship, of the making of friends, of growing old are all in serious disrepair, so much so that one can hardly discuss them without seeming nostalgic. But let's say it anyway: one of the best arguments against having sex on the first date is that it leaves nowhere else to go, thereby short-circuiting the whole process of rituals by which true intimacy and knowledge of another person have to be created. There is a pace at which formality and reserve yield naturally to intimacy; when that pace is forced, the relationship is likely to remain permanently superficial. As for the less highly charged development of friendship, if 'friendliness' and informality are demanded in all encounters, how can real friendship be distinguished from mass-produced copies."

Not merely does this "indiscriminate informality" sweep away all the barriers of decorum and restraint by which we protect the privacy of our intimate selves; it substitutes artificial relationships for real ones. A person unknown to me who insists on calling me "Jonathan"—which, and it is to the point to say so, is not what I am called by most people who know me—is displaying not a genuine interest in me but an indifference to whatever it is in me that might distinguish me from others; which is to say that not merely is the abandonment of the last name a shortcut to false intimacy, it is a denial of the individuality of the person being addressed.

I watched this phenomenon at work a few years ago when, while living in Miami, I made it a point to go out each day for swimming and sun at the apartment complex where I lived. Many of my neighbors were single people and young married couples, and poolside was a natural meeting place. Introductions were commonplace; it was impossible not to hear them. "Hi! I'm

Sherri. This is Rex." "Oh, hi, Sherri! I'm Don, and this is my wife, Christi, and this is Jason and his friend Linda." And there they all were: instant intimates.

What, I used to wonder, ever became of them? Did they chatter on into the evening, comparing notes about fern bars and discos, and end up in bed together—this being the likely culmination of the day's activities—without ever attaching last names to the first ones they had so casually tossed about? Did they ever learn anything about each other that really mattered, that gave them glimpses into each other's characters and personalities more revealing than the disclosure of mutually favored rock musicians and Chinese takeout shops?

Probably not. Probably they managed to achieve the ecstasies of physical union without knowing anything important about each other. By night they gave each other's erogenous zones a first-class workout, and in the morning they awoke as strangers. This is because to deny a person's full name is to deny the person himself. A first name, by itself, is nothing; combine that first name, throw in a middle name or two for good measure, and at once you have an individual, a person with a history. A person, after all, is the sum of all those who went before him, whose lives ultimately produced his own, and it is in his middle and last names that more than a hint of his history and true identity is contained.

But quite apart from that, the insistence on instant and indiscriminate informality gives equal importance—which is to say none at all—to all relationships. It bypasses, and thus eliminates, the gradual process by which evolve personal, as opposed to impersonal, relationships. There was a time, and it was not so long ago, when the abandonment of honorifics meant a significant alteration in a relationship; two people who had theretofore called each other "Mr." declared, by deciding to use first names, that acquaintanceship had become friendship, with all the possibilities for true intimacy and mutual reward that friendship offers. There was also a time when the use of honorifics was a gesture in respect of age, a way of acknowledging that older people have more knowledge and experience of life's joys and sorrows than do young people; for this, custom dictated, they deserved our deference and its symbolic expression.

Those times are gone for good, I suppose, but there is nothing good about it. It is sad indeed to see an old woman called "Mary" by a young receptionist; the latter may think she is kind and "caring," but in truth she is condescending and belittling, denying "Mary" the dignity of age. It is sad as well that the entire culture is now on a first-name basis, so that there is no longer a distinction between one's relationship with a friend and one's dealings with a merchant. This is not intimacy, but self-delusion.

Bundles from Britain

November 11, 1985

Samuel Langhorne Clemens, whose one hundred and fiftieth birthday we celebrate this month, had the final word on royalty, of which we have had enough this month to last several lifetimes. He gave that word to Huck Finn, who as he floated down the river with his friend Jim made the notable—and irrefutable—observation that "all kings is mostly rapscallions, as fur as I can make out," and then added: "All I say is, kings is kings, and you got to make allowances. Take them all around, they're a mighty ornery lot. It's the way they're raised."

A few years before that another notably outspoken American, Ralph Waldo Emerson, had his say on the same subject and reached more or less the same conclusion. In his poem "Boston Hymn" he wrote: "God said, I am tired of kings, / I suffer them no more; / Up to my ear the morning brings / The outrage of the poor." Had Emerson been in Washington this week, heaven knows how he would amend that sentiment; "tired of kings" scarcely begins to say it.

The one consolation is that by the time these words appear the royal visitors will almost—not quite, but almost—be gone, winging their way down to Palm Beach, where, with all due respect, they belong. Soon it will all be over: the tree planting and the wreath laying and the White House dinner and the gallery gala and the (!) J. C. Penney tour and the groupie-packed media reception, not to mention the service at the Washington Cathedral in which the principal objects of worship were He and

She. Soon Washington will be able to get back to its ordinary business, the nature of which is no fit subject for a family newspaper.

But we will be left with what television people, their voices oozing sincerity, like to call Memories, or Magic Moments, or Magically Memorable Moments, all of them preserved on the videotapes of our hearts. For the truth is that our soon-to-be-departed visitors have set us atwitter not because they are royalty but because they are celebrities, and our excitement has much less to do with having the House of Windsor in our midst than with being in the presence of what our visitors would call Glamour. Indeed, the number of Americans who are even aware that this is the House of Windsor probably could convene in a small movie theater; what all of us know is that this is Chuck 'n' Di, once and future monarchs of *People* magazine and all it surveys.

What is amusing about the state of terminal gaga into which we have collapsed is that while we are going berserk at the sheer ecstasy of it all, our royal visitors are taking us to the cleaners. As the *Economist* pointed out last week, the "Treasure Houses of Britain" exhibition at the National Gallery that the famous pair visited yesterday is nothing so much as "a shameless sales pitch for the British heritage," a brilliant piece of public relations designed to lure American tourists to Britain and to encourage them "to extend their next trip to view the treasures hidden in the British countryside."

Who, you may ask, is picking up the freight for this "shameless sales pitch" to which we are so blissfully succumbing? The British taxpayers are shelling out all of $70,000, in the form of staff time at the British Council and a payment—obviously a very small one—to the National Gallery. The rest of the tab is being picked up right here in the colonies: $1.2 million from the Ford Foundation and—you guessed it—$2 million from thee and me, through a special congressional grant. It's as if we went into a grocery store, handed the manager a hundred-dollar bill, and said: "Here. Try and sell me some toilet paper."

 To be sure, when British royalty comes to the United States

it always has something to sell, since in its present condition the British throne is reduced to little more than an agreeably housed and overremunerated public-relations office. Perhaps the most notable royal sales trip to America took place in 1939, when King George VI and Queen Elizabeth paid a call on the Roosevelts and their constituents. Say it for them, though, that their pitch was rather more elevated than the advancement of tourism: They knew that their country would soon be under attack by Nazi Germany, notwithstanding the previous year's capitulation at Munich, and their urgent mission was to renew and intensify American sympathy for all things and causes British.

George and Elizabeth advanced upon the United States in full pomp and circumstance, though they were careful not to overdo it. They seem to have been rather nice people—William Bullitt, advising Franklin Roosevelt about their care and feeding, called them "the little king" and "the little queen"—and the Roosevelts, as was their style, treated them more or less as just folks. Eleanor Roosevelt fretted that "so many people are worried that 'the dignity of our country will be imperiled' by inviting royalty to a picnic, particularly a hot-dog picnic," but a picnic was just what they had: hot dogs and beer, on the lawn at Hyde Park, accompanied by entertainment that the king and queen "were very polite about," according to one present. The visit was probably as happy and successful as any such inherently artificial occasion can be, though at its end Mrs. Roosevelt reflected sadly that "we all knew the king and queen were returning home to face a war."

The only war that He and She will return home to face, after their immersion in the vulgarities and vanities of Palm Beach, will be their unceasing battle against the British press. Such is war, and such is monarchy, in the age of celebrity, that the British throne is reduced to sniping with the tabloids over what goes on in the royal bedroom and whether She has tired of Him, or vice versa, ad infinitum and ad nauseam. Here in America of course we have no time for such matters, and on the subject of Chuck 'n' Di our press has behaved with the utmost decorum, reticence and restraint, and if you believe that you also believe in the tooth fairy.

Oh, well, tomorrow it will be over, at least Washington's end of it. We can go back to the important things—log rolling, influence peddling, social climbing, what have you—and let the royal wedding-cake couple retreat into the mists of Magic Memories. Then perhaps we can even get around to putting these young celebrities in perspective, though as they say Over There: not bloody likely.

Garbage at Georgia

February 17, 1986

The case of Jan Kemp against the University of Georgia has reached a thoroughly satisfactory conclusion, with a $2.6 million judgment in her favor; Kemp, who had been fired as a teacher of remedial education after protesting that the university favored athletes over other students, also will get her job back. But the penalty that the university and its insurers will have to pay, though gratifyingly severe, is hardly the point of the tale. What matters is that the Kemp case forced Georgia's spokesmen to give sworn testimony about the university's attitudes toward the "students" who play football and basketball for it, and that this testimony amounted to a self-inflicted condemnation of the university specifically and intercollegiate athletics generally.

In the history of American higher education, surely a place of honor must be reserved for Fred C. Davison, president of the university, who told the federal district court in Atlanta that it's no big deal if most athletes who play for Georgia do not graduate: "If they leave us being able to read, write, communicate better, we simply have not done them any damage." Even more memorable are the words of Hale Almond, attorney for the two university officials who were defendants in the case, who said of an athlete enrolling at Georgia: "We may not be able to make a university student out of him, but if we can teach him to read and write, maybe he can work at the post office rather than as a garbage man when he gets through with his athletic career."

Perhaps that should be the new rallying cry for the Georgia Bulldogs: "If we can teach him to read and write . . ." Go, 'Dogs!

That's D-O-G-S! Stomp them Cats! That's C-A-T-S! See Spot run. See Spot bounce the ball. The ball is brown. Spot throws the ball into the basket. Go, Spot! S-P-O-T! Spot scores two points. One and one make two. Four minus two makes what? Two! That's two! Ain't college great?

"If we can teach him to read and write . . ." Is it to laugh or to cry? The University of Georgia, like every other institution in the embrace of the National Collegiate Athletic Association, represents itself as a place the principal business of which is the advancement of higher education. Yet the University of Georgia has admitted, through its president and the lawyer representing two of its officials, that it enrolls "students" who need to be taught, in the "remedial developmental studies program," to read and write the English language. This is an institution that has the gall to call itself a "university" yet accepts students who have not mastered the most rudimentary tools of literacy. It does so not to elevate them from the garbage truck to the mail truck, but to make money off them.

For a few hours each week it shovels these eighteen- and nineteen-year-olds into remedial programs where they learn, if they learn anything at all, what they should have been taught in the first year of grammar school, when they were six or seven. Then it trots them onto the football field or basketball court, where they run up and down, occasionally doing injury to themselves, in order to earn money for the university's athletic department and to inflate the egos of its most sports-obsessed alumni. At the end of their four years of eligibility a few—very few—of these "student-athletes" become professional athletes; the rest, some of them only marginally literate after four years of "college," graduate to the garbage truck, or the equivalent thereof.

Many of them, as it happens, are black. Only 4.5 percent of the student body at the University of Georgia is black, but its basketball team is preponderantly black and its football team is heavily so. Interestingly, one of the two officials Kemp sued, himself black, accused her of being a "bigot," a charge she was able to refute handily. But the real truth is that if racism is to be found anywhere it is in the university itself, which recruits black athletes who are academically unprepared, uses them for its own cynical ends and discards them at the end of four years as if they were no more than . . . slaves?

When a "university" has a black population of only 4.5 percent but wildly disproportionate black representation on its big-time athletic teams, what is that university saying to the public at large and blacks specifically? No, it is not saying that it is throwing wide its doors to blacks, helping them gain full and equal admission to American society. It is saying that blacks are good at sports and are most welcome as students at Georgia when they are superior athletes—precisely the reverse of the message being delivered by Jesse Jackson, Arthur Ashe and other black leaders who tell them that precious few kids will find riches as athletes, that education must come first. Not at the University of Georgia, it doesn't; put *that* in your pipe and smoke it.

Okay: Let's lay off the University of Georgia. The only real difference between Georgia and almost everybody else is that Georgia got caught. What goes on at Georgia also goes on, to varying degrees and in varying ways, at just about every school that has committed itself to big-time athletics. With the rarest of exceptions, big-time intercollegiate athletic programs are mockeries of everything that higher education ostensibly stands for—especially, alas, at the major public universities that usually dominate the national rankings.

The football coach at Georgia, Vince Dooley, who is a successful man in his line of work, had this to say about the verdict in the Kemp case: "I would like to reemphasize . . . that throughout the entire ordeal the athletic association has been involved in no wrongdoing, nor been found in violation of any NCAA or institutional regulations." Hey, fellas, our hands are clean—and the stunning truth is that by the standards of big-time intercollegiate athletics, they *are* clean. In NCAA athletics, "clean" means that you haven't gone to jail. Yet.

But in higher education, in a true university, what went on at the University of Georgia was obscene, an affront to every person there who was engaged in serious scholarship, research, teaching and learning. To keep its fat-cat alumni happy, the University of Georgia thumbed its nose at the very educational standards it claims to uphold. Its administrators may feel unfairly singled out—the eminently quotable Fred C. Davison told the court its teams could not "disarm unilaterally" in the dog-eat-dog world of the NCAA—but the university got just what it deserved: an ineradicable stain on its reputation.

Of Thee I Sing, Baby

March 10, 1986

The centennial celebration for the Statue of Liberty is almost four months away, but there's no need to hold your breath about what kind of event it will be. The program described last week by the chairman of the celebration committee is a paradigmatic example of American schlock, four days of glitz and glitter that likely will leave poor Miss Liberty blushing from torch to toe. By the end of those four days, the French may be demanding that we ship the old girl back.

One need only be told the name of the committee's chairman to realize what lies in store. The gentleman chosen for the job is none other than David Wolper, the Hollywood producer whose greatest gift to his country—up to now, that is—was the opening and closing schlock for the 1984 Los Angeles Olympic Games, or, as Peter Ueberroth and ABC Sports insisted on calling them, "The Games of the XXIII Olympiad." Wolper pulled out all the stops, assembling a monument to execrable taste by contrast with which a Super Bowl halftime is a Dürer woodcut and the Grammy awards a Mozart quintet.

It seems, though, that for the lady in New York harbor Wolper is going to outdo even himself, if that is humanly possible. At the cost of a mere $8 million—a drop in the bucket to big-bucks Reaganites—he will put on a show guaranteed to leave P. T. Barnum and Mike Todd spinning in their graves with envy. For starters, on July 3 the president will be joined aboard the USS *John F. Kennedy* by three thousand fat cats, three thousand journalists, an orchestra of one hundred musicians and a choir of one thousand. At the press of a presidential switch, the *Washington Post* reported last week, "a beam of light will cross the harbor, slowly steal up the statute amid a swell of music, and finally illuminate Miss Liberty as the choir bursts into song."

As Wolper said, "It's going to be quite a moving moment." Not to mention a memorable moment and a magic moment and a special moment. In the Age of Moments we will have to reserve a precious place for this one, which surely will be just a teeny bit more memorable than such previous moments—all preserved forever and a day on videotape, all celebrated in lavish hyperbole and breathless rapture by the high priests of videoland—as a slam dunkeroo by Doctor J or a spin and a grin by Mary Lou Retton.

But that moving moment is only the tip of Wolper's iceberg. Fifteen hundred new citizens are to be sworn in by Chief Justice Warren Burger on Ellis Island, and forty thousand others at simultaneous ceremonies elsewhere. There will be fireworks, cannons, tall ships, small ships, cheering crowds of millions—all of this on July 3. In the days to follow there will be concerts by the likes of Johnny Cash and—the event certainly would be incomplete without him—Barry Manilow; appearances by stars from the wonderful world of sport, Mary Lou Retton being, of course, prominent among them; and, the crowning touch, a party at the Meadowlands attended by myriad stars and starlets from the even more wonderful world of movies and TV.

Makes you proud to be an American, doesn't it? This is what they fought for at Bunker Hill, froze for at Valley Forge, triumphed for at Yorktown: Barry Manilow, Mary Lou Retton, the Harlem Globetrotters. But, hey, Wolper, make sure you don't leave anyone out. What about Joan Rivers? Liberace? Mr. T? Leo Buscaglia? Wayne Newton? Tiny Tim? John McEnroe? Ed McMahon? Bert Parks? Judith Krantz? Christo? Redd Foxx? Leona Helmsley? Sylvester Stallone? Donald Trump? Don Johnson? Reggie Jackson? John Houseman? Billy Martin? George Steinbrenner? Barbra Streisand? Sammy Davis, Jr.? Barbara Walters? The San Diego Chicken?

Listen: If Wolper is going to go all the way for Miss Liberty, he's got to go *all* the way. No holding back on this one, no tiptoeing around the edges. Firecrackers and cannons aren't enough; this calls for an air force flyby, a Pete Rozelle special. It's all well and good to have the Boston Pops, but we need Mantovani and Al Hirt and 101 Strings. If what we're going to have is bad taste, then let's make certain it's *bad* taste.

There are, to be sure, a few malcontents and spoilsports out there who think it's inappropriate to celebrate the centennial of the Statue of Liberty with "celebrities." They have the odd, if not heretical, notion that flag waving and chest thumping are not what the Statue of Liberty is about, that the emotions most suitable to the occasion are gratitude and humility. They think that a rhinestone-cowboy binge at the Meadowlands somehow is not exactly what Emma Lazarus had in mind when she wrote about "your tired, your poor," about "wretched refuse," about "the homeless, tempest-tost"—about those who, in another time, the Statue of Liberty welcomed to these shores.

Innocent fools that they are, these people actually think the centennial of the Statue of Liberty is no excuse for telling ourselves, as in these Reagan years we have taken such self-congratulatory pleasure in doing, how wonderful we are. They have the preposterous idea that a three-ring circus, with the Great Communicator as ringmaster, does not exactly rise to the occasion; that tall ships are indeed vivid reminders of how millions of immigrants crossed the oceans, but that an aircraft carrier stuffed with fat cats and high rollers is a wee bit out of place.

What do they know? Obviously they don't know that in the land of show biz, every occasion, no matter how solemn, must be inflated to the outer limits of garishness and thereby rendered wholly trivial. They don't know that there's a buck to be made out there, especially when the buck comes wrapped around a symbol of national identity as potent as Miss Liberty. They don't know that what matters now is not the meaning of the ceremony, but the ceremony itself: the glitter, the glitz, the empty self-satisfaction masquerading as patriotism.

The truth is that the Wolper celebration is as exemplary a

manifestation of the times as could be manufactured, and therefore exactly appropriate for the new, improved Miss Liberty. In our public life—political, social, cultural—substance no longer matters; style is all, and the style of the moment is vulgar, flashy and smug. To hell with "huddled masses yearning to breathe free"; send in the clowns.

Cooking the Evidence

June 16, 1986

The case of the women's movement against Rosalind Rosenberg is a deeply disturbing example of what can happen when ideological orthodoxy is allowed to take priority over scholarly integrity. Rosenberg, a professor of history at Barnard College in New York, is being widely and quite maliciously vilified among feminist scholars for having the effrontery to take a public position that they regard as injurious to women's interests; their attack is proof positive that they have their priorities wildly out of whack.

The controversy grows out of a sex discrimination suit filed by the Equal Employment Opportunity Commission against Sears, Roebuck & Company. The suit, nearly a decade in the making, alleged that Sears had not promoted women employees within its sales staff to a degree commensurate with their proportion of its work force. Sears contested the suit, claiming that considerations other than sex discrimination produced the imbalance between promotions of men and women, and brought a number of "expert" witnesses to the stand to endorse its position.

One of these was Rosenberg, who agreed to speak on Sears' behalf after other prominent historians rejected its overtures. She testified that in seeking jobs women have attempted to strike a balance between their need for income and their desire to meet family responsibilities, with the result that many women have been willing to accept lower-paying jobs that permit them to spend time with their families. She also testified that some of the sales jobs at Sears required an expertise on certain items—she mentioned aluminum siding and furnaces—with which women are often unfamiliar.

Sears won the case, but in academic-feminist circles, Rosenberg lost. She has been severely criticized in several academic journals, including a couple devoted to feminist revisionism, and a number of her fellow historians have spoken harshly about her. One called her testimony "an immoral act." Another put it this way: "The issue is purely this. You would not lie in your testimony, but you also would not say or write something as a historian solely to hurt a group of people. And the consequences of Rosalind's testimony can be interpreted that way." Still another weighed in as follows:

"This was one of the first times women historians have found their scholarship to be of policy-making significance. And the symbolic step of a self-described feminist getting on the stand to testify against the EEOC and for Sears astonished people. It's not that what she said was wrong. It's that she used it for a purpose many people would quarrel with."

One can only wonder how well these people sleep at night. They are scholars, at least one of them well known outside the history departments, yet what they are saying in these minced words is that the obligation to feminist orthodoxy is higher than the obligation to scholarly integrity. Their counsel to Rosenberg is not to state the historical truth as her researches have led her to understand it, but to keep silent about the truth if it might, in the judgment of the feminist thought-control police, do damage to the feminist cause.

Perhaps these women need a refresher course in the words of another feminist. "I cannot and will not cut my conscience to fit this year's fashions," Lillian Hellman told the House Un-American Activities Committee three and a half decades ago. She may well have been wallowing in characteristic self-righteousness and theatricality, but all the same she was right: A person of conscience does not alter his or her views in order to meet the

 shifting demands of political fashion. Yet that is precisely what the academic feminists are demanding that Rosenberg—and, by implication, any other scholar claiming to be a feminist—agree to do. How else is one to interpret the resolution, passed last winter by a committee of female historians, asserting that "as feminist scholars we have a responsibility not to allow our scholarship to be used against the interests of women struggling for equity in our society?"

So much for academic freedom: Shut your mouth and toe the line, because the end justifies the means. They may call it feminism, but it sounds for all the world like totalitarianism. In the little world of the academic feminists, speech is free only so long as it serves the interests of the Cause. If what you believe, or what you interpret history as saying, runs contrary to those interests, then it is your obligation to keep your silence. That this is merely one form of lying seems to bother no one.

Almost no one, that is. Catherine Clinton, an exceptionally promising young scholar, has this to say: "I'm someone who calls myself a feminist and owes my origins to the women's movement. But it would be throwing away my integrity to let politics determine my scholarship, and it would undermine the integrity of women's history." Carl Degler, whose concern with women in history predates the current phase of the feminist movement, says: "History is a discipline in which we try to discover the truth as we understand it. It's possible to disagree on interpretation, but that's part of professional activity."

Precisely. In history, as in literature or philosophy or any other discipline in which there is no such thing as absolute truth, disagreement is a given. If anything, disagreement is the yeast by which vigorous debate among historians is fermented, debate that may lead them to a deeper understanding of the past than their individual investigations could yield. Responsible historians, such as C. Vann Woodward, seek out and welcome debate. "Granted that criticism involves differences of opinion," Woodward has written, "so does any worthwhile colleagueship. The adversarial part of the critic's role is certainly present, but it is, or should be, concerned with the discovery of error. . . . And presumably both the critic and the criticized share as their common goal the pursuit of truth."

Not, however, in academic-feminist circles. There the search is not for what is true but for what is ideologically correct. The concern of these "scholars" is with selectively mining that past in order to trump up what passes for "evidence" of grievances and wrongs against women; if what they find does not suit their purposes, they quietly, and guiltlessly, set it aside. The Cause comes above all: above the evidence, above truth, above—how can one escape this conclusion?—integrity.

They call this "history," but it's history of a most self-serving and selective kind. No honorable historian—female or male, feminist or chauvinist, liberal or conservative—would dream of practicing it. And no reputable history department would grant either appointments or tenure to "scholars" who so openly and flagrantly advocate the abandonment of scholarly principles.

Buzzword for the Eighties

September 1, 1986

Batten down the hatches, boys, we're in for a siege. A new buzzword is in the air, and it looks as though we're going to have a fair storm before things quiet down. This storm may last awhile, because it revolves around one of those Mom, baseball and apple pie buzzwords that people in public life dearly love to exploit as much as they can. That it raises an issue far more complex than any of them have thus far acknowledged is hardly the point; the whole purpose of buzzwords is to disguise complexity, not to unravel it.

The word is "values." It was given currency by William Bennett, the secretary of education, a man of serious purpose if somewhat elephantine style who has been using the bully pulpit provided by his office to preach the lesson that schools should teach "values." Now, leaping in from the opposite side of the ideological divide, comes Mario Cuomo, the evangelical governor of New York, with almost exactly the same message. In a conversation with reporters aboard the gubernatorial airplane, Cuomo said last week that he will soon issue a pronunciamento on the subject, and gave more than a hint of its character when he said:

"When you have kids in elementary school and you don't teach anything about values, I suspect the message you're sending is that there are no values. What's happened in the last twenty years is that we've said, 'No values—we'll teach no values.' It's all produced a vacuum. I don't think we're teaching any moral structure in any formal way. . . . What is the value of the person? What is dignity? These are things to be talked about. What is the obligation of the people around you to your brothers and sisters?"

Cuomo emphasized that he was not talking about religious values—though he quoted Scripture in citing "love thy neighbor" as one value the schools should teach—and he said the schools should stay away from such private matters as sexual standards. He acknowledged as well the risk of "sounding religious, moralistic, unctuous," but insisted that teaching values is "extremely important" and that "we've got to give it a try." Precisely how we should do so presumably is to be revealed in the speech that Cuomo, candidate for reelection this fall and presumptive candidate for president two years later, eventually will deliver.

All of which is well and good, except that it begs the central question: What are "values"? In certain countries, the question can be answered with little difficulty: racially and culturally homogenous societies, totalitarian states, nations in which church and state are intimately connected. In those countries there often can be near unanimity about the values citizens hold most dear, and they can be taught in the schools without posing any threat to civic comity.

But in the United States, the most heterogeneous nation in the world, one man's values can be another man's anathema. As Ralph Ellison has written, "the drama of American social hierarchy" is "that combat of civility, piety and tradition" among the minority groups to which all of us belong—groups that, among their many differences, often disagree about values. This is as true of the big, universal values—those that fall into the mainstream of the American ethos—as it is of personal and private ones; disagreements arise about important particulars even when we can agree on generalities.

Take, as a case in point, love of country. Most of us would agree that we should love our country and support it in peace and war—mercifully, the native anti-Americanism of the sixties and early seventies seems a thing of the past—but when it comes to how we do so, that's where the squabbling begins. Some people are low-key patriots who think the Pledge of Allegiance has no place in the classroom; others wear their patriotism on their sleeves and expect the schools to do likewise, with the full panoply of pledges and anthems and similar expressions of patriotic zeal. Who is to say which side is "right," which side expresses an "American value"? Not I, for one—and not, most Americans probably would agree, Bill Bennett or Mario Cuomo.

The problem with values is that in a country where freedom of expression is a right upon which we all (more or less) agree, people insist on expressing themselves. When I was an impressionable ten-year-old I spent an entire school year—five days a week, six or seven hours a day—in the presence of a redoubtable and terrifying teacher who had values coming out of her ears and who had conceived it her life's mission to insinuate those values into every lesson she taught. Unfortunately, though, her values were quite at odds with those upon which my parents were attempting to raise me, which had much to do with my subsequent departure for six miserable years as a preparatory school scholarship boy.

But in sending me off to private schools, my parents were able to choose places that taught values in which they themselves believed. It is a choice made regularly by millions of American parents, at virtually every economic level, who send their children to parochial schools or fundamentalist academies or other private institutions that teach values as well as academic lessons. But in the polyglot world of the public schools, this simply can't be done. The public schools are open to children from families who embrace all values, and thus the inescapable conclusion is that the public schools must embrace none—except, obviously, those related to educational standards and norms of student behavior.

To say this is not to say that the issue raised by Bennett, Cuomo and others is frivolous; quite to the contrary. The sense that the country is morally rudderless is well founded and disturbing. But throwing the problem onto the schools is hardly the answer. Already we demand that they serve *in loco parentis* in more areas than they can handle, from driver's education to sex education. Does it really make any sense to add still further to their burden, to insist that they provide the answers to questions of values upon which we mature adults cannot agree?

The truth of it is that if the country is indeed in a crisis of values, we adults are to blame for it. The most important lessons children learn about values are those taught at home, by the counsel and behavior of their parents; if children are poorly reared at home, it is a tall order for the schools to correct the damage. Children also learn values from the language and behavior of public officials, but the values now emanating from official Washington are not those any self-respecting parent would want his or her children to learn—nor, for that matter, are those embraced by most public figures in the business world, or in popular culture. We'd best try setting a better example ourselves before we ask the schoolteachers to do the job for us.

Oh, What a Beautiful Child

September 29, 1986

"There's a big, bouncing, healthy new market out there," the full-page advertisement in *Manhattan, inc.* proclaimed last week. "It's today's new parents who want the very best for their children—in fashion, food, schools, play—in life. And finally, there's a magazine that delivers. *Child.* A big, beautiful magazine of style, created by the market it is devoted to."

Ah, yes: *Child.* "For parents who only want the best for their children." Or, to put it perhaps a trifle more accurately, for parents who only want the best for themselves. Upper-middle-class parvenus have at last discovered children, and *Child* is the entirely predictable result: a magazine that will help train them in conspicuous display of their children, just as they already display their European automobiles and Caribbean vacations and Upper East Side condominiums and Pierre Cardin carry-ons.

When the history of the decline of the republic is written, surely a chapter will be reserved for *Child,* now at newsstands—selected newsstands, no doubt, in all the very best neighborhoods—in its "Premiere" issue. A spinoff of a European magazine called *Taxi* ("Europe's hottest magazine has arrived in the United States. It's fast paced and devoted to fashion, style, people, trends and leisure living"), *Child* is slick and glossy and drop-dead chic. *Manhattan, inc.* was the perfect place to announce its arrival: Surrounded by all those adoring articles about *arriviste* financiers and climbing socialites, *Child*'s advertisement was right at home.

On its premiere issue's cover a freckled girl gazes out at us, her oh-so-cute snaggletooth just the last word in adorability. She's wearing a Dior houndstooth Chesterfield coat (about $200 at Saks, Nieman-Marcus and Bloomingdale's) and a ring on her finger (price not provided). The coat's the perfect touch, because *Child* is a magazine for the people to whom Saks, Nieman-Marcus and Bloomingdale's are the new American cathedrals; on every page, *Child* sings them the Hallelujah Chorus of self-indulgence.

Children aren't children in *Child;* they're little objects to be dressed in expensive clothes and set out for the world to admire—or, again to put it more accurately, for the world to admire the people who dressed them. As the editor in chief of *Child* puts it in her letter of greetings: "Our children dress beautifully because it's important for their self-esteem and our sense of style." It's the latter, make no bones about it, that matters to *Child:* the "sense of style" of its adult readers.

Or, as an advertisement for Jet Set clothing puts it: "We Believe That Children Should Be Seen As Well As Heard," and as Baby Dior would have it: "Make a French Impression." The editor's letter may claim that there has been a "cultural shift from the me generation to the next generation," but the message *Child* sends its readers is: you, you, you. It unabashedly represents itself as the natural successor to those "special magazines [that] cheer us on and help us dress for success, invest our money, entertain, get married, stay fit, and design wonderful houses." Having a child, in the world of *Child,* is an act not of family but of self: another step along the path toward—forgive my use of the vogue vulgarities—an upscale life-style.

But having a child can be something of a nuisance in the upscale life-style. Never fear, *Child* is here: "Life has never been more rewarding, more complex, more hectic. *Child* responds to our needs by doing the homework for us and leaving us more time to spend with our families. . . . *Child* gives parents more joy and less bother by featuring the best children's clothes and home furnishings, the latest reports on education, health, the arts, book and film reviews, top-of-the-line baby products, and more." Just ask *Child* and you too can have it: parenthood without pain.

Of course it takes a bit of grease. A nanny will run you $180 to $350 a week, though even nanny comes with her own problems; a mother of twins confessed ("while stashing two color-coded pacifiers into a diaper bag") that "I used to worry about losing my husband to another woman. Now I'm more afraid of losing my *nanny* to another woman." If you want the kid to look like a real man, you've got to dig deep: $180 for a Marc Ariana leather jacket with sherpa lining, $130 for a Polo sweater, $35 for a chambray work shirt and $42 for leather-trimmed jeans, both by Guess at Saks. And then there's lunch:

"Who else but Mary Emmerling would 'design' her daughter's lunch with the same care and feeding she brings to her best-selling books on country style? And why not. Her spiced apple candles and wooden watermelons have decorated many a pine-plank kitchen table. Daughter Samantha just *loves* her heart-shaped cucumber and watercress sandwich with herbed mayonnaise. The acceptable fruit salad is a mix of sliced kiwi, raspberries and green apples. The chocolate chip cookies are made from Nestlé's frozen toll house packages. The high point of this lunch, which takes one hour to prepare, is the fresh lemonade with lemon slices."

If that doesn't put the kid on what another article calls the academic "fast track," nothing will. But give the devil his due: The author of the article about academics wisely counsels that "parents are pushing their children too hard and too fast into academic and other skills—and for no good reason," and quotes an educational researcher as saying: "All this heavy pressure in academics on middle-class kids does no one any good. If anything, it's helping kids lose a year of their childhood."

The point is well taken, but it scarcely seems to have registered with the editors of *Child.* Though they make the obligatory gestures toward the innocence of childhood, their principal emphasis is upon childhood as miniature adulthood. There is far less emphasis on toys in *Child*—they are the subject of only one article, about Lego blocks, which "have redeeming educational value"—than there is on finances, manners, grooming, education and clothes. Above all, clothes. *Child* is to children's clothes what *Vogue* is to adults': obsessive, encyclopedic and *au courant.* In its advertisements and in its editorial material, the dress-for-success theme predominates; but it's the parents' success, not the children's, that's foremost in mind.

No doubt *Child* will have its day in the sun and then go the way of all those other magazines pegged to the passing fancies of the upwardly mobile, so even upon the occasion of its birth we can look forward with pleasure to its demise. But for now there it is, soon to make its way onto the coffee tables of the very best people, glossy evidence that in the upscale life-style, even a child is merely an *objet de vanité.*

Why Johnny Can't Write

December 8, 1986

In the department of non-news, last week's disclosure that American schoolchildren do not know how to write surely deserves a place all to itself. Is anybody out there actually shocked by the declaration, made by something called the National Assessment of Educational Progress, that "most students, majority and minority alike, are unable to write adequately except in response to the simplest of tasks"?

The report did, to be sure, provoke the ususal expressions of dismay. Secretary of Education Bennett, under whose auspices the study was undertaken, said unoriginally that "we can and should do better," and Albert Shanker, president of the American Federation of Teachers, managed to work himself into something of a frenzy. "Before us we have a very disturbing, indeed a shocking report," he said. "It goes to the very heart of what our aims in education are about." But that was just about that; the silence in other quarters was deafening for the simple reason that nothing genuinely newsworthy had been discovered.

This is not to make light of the study's findings, which are both serious and dispiriting, but to note that they merely tell us what we have known all along. The skill of writing—not to mention the art—never has been held in especially high regard among Americans, but its standing in the age of television and technology is especially low, with the entirely predictable consequence that it is not being taught competently in the schools. Like the Supreme Court, the schools follow the election returns;

the returns tell them that writing does not rank high among the skills we expect them to teach.

The schools, in the American view, exist not to provide an education in the traditional sense of the word, but to equip students with the necessary tools for adult careers and for coping effectively in adult society. Writing is regarded as such a tool only to the extent that it is necessary for filling out applications and forms, for recording data and for communicating information. But writing as something to be mastered—a skill in its own right—is, and always has been, given short shrift.

"American students can write at a minimal level," last week's report says, "but cannot express themselves well enough to ensure that their writing will accomplish the intended." True enough; but it is also true of adult Americans as well, of all classes, races and income groups. We learn enough about writing in order to accomplish what we think we need of it, and then we lose interest in it—an observation confirmed by the report, which noted that while 57 percent of fourth graders said they like to write, only 39 percent of eleventh graders said the same.

Certainly there have always been Americans who care about writing, and Americans who write with clarity and elegance, but we have never had a tradition of writing excellence comparable to England's. To an extent this is a matter of class: The British upper class and gentry, educated at the public (i.e., private) secondary schools, are expected to write well and are taught to do so. But skillful writing—forceful, lucid, witty, persuasive—is almost as common in British culture as it is rare in American; the reason presumably is that the British are brought up to respect and value writing as a skill to be mastered for its own sake, and Americans are not.

To see the difference, one need only read the two countries' journalism and popular fiction. With the rarest of exceptions, the most that can be said of the prose in American newspapers and best-selling novels is that it is competent; too often it is riddled with malapropisms, infelicities and just plain howlers. British journalism, by contrast, is written with suavity and flair even in the yellow press, and British popular novels often startle the American reader with their smooth, graceful prose.

This is said not in a spirit of raving Anglophilia, an ailment with which I have never been afflicted, but as a simple matter of fact. Whatever the faults of British society, they are in some measure redeemed by the value it places on good writing, not merely in the press and in public discourse, but in private correspondence and business dealings as well. Americans are too busy getting ahead—which is, of course, one of our society's greatest strengths—to care about whether their writing does anything more than get the job done; and since just about everybody writes poorly, or indifferently, it doesn't take much to do that.

There is absolutely no reason to believe, or even to hope, that this will change. We can spend the next century forming committees and issuing reports, bemoaning this and deploring that, but none of the hoopla will alter the basic conditions of American society. The most important of these is that writing is no longer essential to the exchange of information. We don't write letters anymore; we talk on the telephone. We do read newspapers and magazines—though circulation has failed to keep up with population growth—but our primary sources of information and entertainment are technological: television and radio, video and tape recorders, computers and sound systems.

These are not media in which capable writing is important or even necessary. At times they may require scripts, but a well-crafted script is one that imitates the patterns of speech, not one that follows the dictates of formal prose. Beyond that, these are media that place greatest value on spontaneity and informality, little if any on discipline and structure. Radio and television, movies and videos, are instruments of talk and sound; prose stylists need not apply—and since these are the media of the foreseeable future, prose stylists will be ever fewer and ever less in demand.

Those are facts that no commission or report can circumvent. They are compounded, furthermore, by the inescapable reality that Americans are not regular readers and that most of what they do read is badly written. It is all well and good to deplore this—and, just for the record, I herewith do so—but no amount of lamentation is going to change a thing. Certainly the schools can and should be encouraged to place greater emphasis on "communications skills," as the educationists have it, but in writing as in everything else, we cannot expect the schools to correct ills that are pandemic in the greater society. Americans will want to write well only if they believe that it will profit them to do so; but the message society sends them is that minimal competence—at most—is all they need.

The Lauren "Look"

December 15, 1986

If it is the peculiar genius of Americans constantly to reinvent themselves, then surely Ralph Lauren is the All-American boy. This fabricator of clothing and domestic artifacts, who grew up in the Bronx and changed his name from Lifshitz when he was sixteen years old, has managed the not-inconsiderable feat of transforming himself into the embodiment of Edwardian tweediness and has made an immodest fortune in the process. Now, according to the *New York Times,* his influence has grown so large that at this Christmas season the Manhattan shopping district has been transformed into a virtual museum in his honor.

"It's beginning to look a lot like Christmas in New York," the *Times* reported last week. "And Christmas in the nation's largest marketplace is beginning to look a lot like Ralph Lauren." The business-section story went on to catalogue not merely the contents of Lauren's five-story emporium on Madison Avenue, where gentry *manqué* can purchase all the necessary accouterments of false status, but those of other establishments that are desperately trying to imitate the Lauren "look": Descamps, where one can obtain sheets patterned with ducks and geese, and Altman's, which has an "English country feel" in its windows on Fifth Avenue.

All the world of fashion has prostrated itself at Lauren's feet, which is a nice twist of fate considering that Lauren has never really been a fashion insider. As Witold Rybczynski points out in his brilliant book *Home: A Short History of an Idea:* "Unlike

Cardin and Saint Laurent, whose careers were founded in the exclusive dress salons, Lauren was never a couturier; from the beginning he was concerned with mass-produced clothing, and so he acquired an understanding of popular instead of elite tastes. His renown as a designer has been the result of his commercial success, not vice versa."

Though some might argue that Lauren has a genius for design, his real genius—if that is the word for it—is for connecting his own upwardly mobile longings with those of the mass market. Just as the boy from the Bronx wants to be a British gentleman, so millions of other Americans want to be something they are not—and are prepared to spend ludicrous amounts of money in the hope of transforming themselves. The Lauren "look" has relatively little to do with style as fashion, but everything to do with style as summarized in that loathsome coinage, "life-style."

Lauren seems to have a visceral understanding of the insecurities about class and place that plague so many Americans, and he has made himself rich by providing the trappings through which "image," if not actuality, can be altered. What he sells is instant gentility. As Rybczynski notes, "You can now put on a Lauren dressing gown, slip on a pair of Lauren slippers, shower with Lauren soap, dry with a Lauren towel, walk across a Lauren rug, glance at the Lauren wallpaper, and slip between Lauren sheets, beneath a Lauren comforter, to sip warm milk from a Lauren glass." Spend an hour in a Lauren emporium, and you can walk away more royalist than the queen: You too can be Jeremy Irons.

But this "look" is not for everyone. To wear the Lauren label—always, need it be said, prominently if not ostentatiously displayed—one must come well equipped with cash or credit. But that, of course, is the point. Lauren may sell his products across a wide range of social and even economic classes, but his primary market is among the *arrivistes:* those who have come lately to wealth, or an approximation thereof, and are now attempting to fashion the appropriate "life-style" for themselves.

If you've just leveraged your way into a duplex on the Upper East Side and know how neither it nor you should be accoutered, Lauren is the man for you; from him you can purchase instant image.

But because it all has to do with money and image, there's a furtive desperation to Laurenization. Lauren may radiate "comfort," as Rybczynski suggests, but beneath the argyled veneer beats an insecure pulse. No doubt there are exceptions, but Lauren's customers are not to the manor, or the manner, born; in styling themselves in his aggressively casual wares, they are trying to take shortcuts to the manor, and the manner. That is why Lauren places such emphasis, in his genuinely egregious advertisements, on clothing that has been, in effect, preworn; the *Brideshead* look is one of rumpled ease, so the ever-obliging Lauren sells the rumples built-in.

Nothing so vividly demonstrates the essential fraudulence of the Lauren "look" as the aforesaid advertisements, which customarily are published in the most prominent pages of the *The New York Times Magazine*, the medium through which the fashion industry addresses itself to the outside world. Featuring models of unintentionally self-parodic "British" appearance—imagine Peter O'Toole with all the blood sucked out and you've got the picture—these advertisements are so shamelessly "casual" and so aggressively "upper crust" that they can appeal only to persons whose own sense of what is casual and good-mannered is entirely unshaped by experience.

"Reverence for the past has become so strong," Rybczynski writes, "that when traditions do not exist, they are frequently invented." The Lauren "look" is, in effect, an invented "tradition." It is ersatz English, ersatz aristocratic, ersatz status. In that respect to be sure it is entirely American, since the only real upper crust in this country is the moneyed class, and since money is the standard by which most American values ultimately are decided. The money is what really counts; the only difference between a parvenu in a shark-skin suit and a parvenu in a Lauren blazer is that the latter has pretensions.

People are quite entitled to their affectations, needless to say, and if Lauren has been able to make a fortune by catering to the human longing for advanced social status, more power to him. But we should not allow him to confuse actual with contrived elegance. People who were to the manor born, odious though some of them certainly may be, do not need to display designer labels or polo player insignia in order to tell the world who they are; their status, such as it is, is a matter of fact rather than ostentation. Anyone who deludes himself into believing that when he puts on his Polo shirt he is displaying his own "English country" casualness is living in Fool's Paradise.

But if Manhattan at this Christmastime "is beginning to look a lot like Ralph Lauren," that is entirely appropriate. More than at any time in its history, Manhattan is overrun with aggressive, avaricious strivers whose sole goals in life are money and status. In the Lauren "look," they look just like themselves.

The New Pestilence

January 12, 1987

If we are to believe the sociologists and futurologists and other ologists engaged in the dubious business of telling us what tomorrow may or may not bring, ours is soon to become a nation of stay-at-homes, burrowed away in our home offices doing work in solitude that we now do in the company of others. The future, the seers would have us believe, is home-based computers attached, via telephone lines and modems, to distant data centers. But that is only part of it; the future is also Colleen.

Yes, Colleen. She called late one afternoon last week and asked for Mrs. Yardley. That should have been giveaway enough, inasmuch as Mrs. Yardley does not call herself Mrs. Yardley, but in all innocence I asked if she was the Colleen who lives down the street. No, she replied, she was Colleen So-and-so. Well then, I asked, what did she want with Mrs. Yardley? She wanted, need it be said, money, in this case money laundered through magazine subscriptions that was ultimately to go, she claimed, to a program for those children who are described as "special." Politely but firmly, I wished her a good day and rang off.

Colleen, like all the other Colleens huddled at their telephones, drearily working their way through the pages of the telephone directory, is a daily reality of the new work order. For anyone who works at home, telephone solicitation is as much a part of the routine as the word processor, the typewriter or whatever machine one uses to do one's business. Not merely that, but it is a reality the dimensions of which seem to be growing, steadily and inexorably, from occasional nuisance to ubiquity.

This conclusion is drawn from empirical observation. I have been a member of the home office work force for nearly a dozen years and can report from increasingly painful experience that the volume of telephone solicitations has increased markedly during that period. The original culprits, in my experience at least, were a handful of organizations soliciting used clothing and housewares to be sold, they claimed, for the benefit of disabled veterans. We went so far as to permit them to pick up a few elderly items of clothing, thereby sparing us a trip to Goodwill, but promptly ceased this munificence when we learned upon inquiry that some of these organizations are not nonprofit and are not considered by the Internal Revenue Service to be of a charitable nature.

We stopped giving, but they didn't stop calling. "Take us off your list," we'd tell them, but a month later, having worked their way through the phone book, they'd be back on the wire. A few choice words, spoken at impressive volume, had no better effect. Now, at the sound of voices that have become as recognizable, and as unpleasant, as those of Henry Kissinger and John Houseman, we hang up the receiver without a word. But still they call, and call, and call—and no doubt will call the day I am summoned to the great phone booth in the sky.

The police call, too, and the firemen: retired police and firemen, actually, but when they solicit for their annual charities they are not loath to imply that their good causes have the approval of the respective departments in question and that donations are evidence of good citizenship. They don't get a nickel. Neither does the leukemia lady, whose cause may be worthy but whose manner leaves much to be desired; she clearly was offended when told that if she wished to solicit my attentions, or my bank account, or anything else, she could do so through the mail.

Indeed, these disembodied voices are remarkably quick to

take affront should their prey express indignation, or even polite dismay, at having their work and privacy thus interrupted. No doubt making these calls is monotonous work, and a day of it must drum up a lot of unwelcome abuse, but that comes, as they say, with the territory. For a telephone solicitor to take offense at a prospective customer's irritation is approximately as justifiable as for a television pitchman to upbraid his audience for pressing fast forward.

The solicitors come in all voices and all causes. Though most of the callers are women, the occasional male chimes in from time to time; so too does the occasional tape recorder, as soliciting organizations have begun to learn that the human touch can be cheaper when computerized. Not merely do these callers want donations for the retarded and the police and the victims of leukemia; they also want our views on matters political, our purchasing patterns on various items at large in the marketplace, our participation as neighborhood agents in one fund drive or another. Mainly, though, they just want our money.

This, if little else, distinguishes them from the Jehovah's Witnesses, who want our souls and come right to the front door to get them. They make their regular rounds through the neighborhood, immediately recognizable because they are the only people afoot who are dressed in Sunday best, ringing each doorbell in hopes of drawing the unfortunate person who answers it into conversation about God and the hereafter. Those are heavy subjects for a working day, and so the apostles must be turned away. They are decent, worthy people, and no doubt their cause is good; they are also pests.

Whether they arrive by foot or by phone, those who enter unbidden the houses of persons whom they do not know seem to imagine themselves performing a service of sorts, whether to charity or to Mammon or to God. Nothing could be further from the truth. They may be perfectly nice people, and one can certainly sympathize with those who must support themselves by telephone solicitation because handicaps or illnesses make them shut-ins, but the only real businesses they are engaged in are invasion of privacy and interruption of work. Perhaps their calls are welcomed by the lonely or the bored; but to anyone trying to put in a day's work, they are a nuisance and a distraction.

Not only that, but there seems no way to eliminate them. Acquiring an unlisted number might be one, but it's not for me; a person who expresses opinions in public ought to be available to the public for dissent and debate, so I'm in the phone book. Leaving the answering machine on all day might be another, but that's rude to one's friends and business associates; besides, ever since the days when free-lance work was an important part of my income, and the phone often meant work, I've been constitutionally incapable of letting ringing phones ring. So what it comes down to is that if Colleen's calling, I'm answering; and if there is one certainty in this brave new world, it's that Colleen will call again.

Andy Warhol, R.I.P.

March 2, 1987

Andy Warhol was a paradigmatic figure of his age, which speaks volumes—none of them flattering—about the age. If art reveals the artist, then what are we to say of Warhol? His "art," however amusing and clever some of it may be, is callow, utterly devoid of seriousness or larger purpose. And if the public figure discloses the private man, then what again are we to say of Warhol? His much publicized life was dedicated, quite without shame, to the pursuit of wealth and fame, to flattery of the rich and indifference to virtually everyone else.

Perhaps it was really otherwise; speaking ill of the dead gives no pleasure, especially when as in Warhol's case death comes prematurely, so it is nice to imagine that beneath Warhol's cynical, avaricious exterior beat the heart of a good man and true. But, wishful thinking to the contrary notwithstanding, appearances do not often deceive. The Warhol we saw in the galleries and the gossip columns seems, on all the evidence, to have been *echt* Warhol. As was once said of a Hollywood eminence: Deep down he was shallow.

But shallowness, in the age of Warhol, has its rewards. In the venal, profoundly commercialized world of big-time contemporary art, what matters is not excellence but trendiness, and for a quarter century Warhol was trendier than anyone else; he was always, to use one of the age's more odious phrases, "ahead of the curve." No thought or reflection seems to have gone into his "art" beyond a rather vague and ex post facto urge to satirize; its dominant impulse was to work the market, to tap the deep wells of cash that keep the art world turning. Like Truman Capote, Warhol knew how to bleed the "patrons" of fast-lane New York for all they were worth; unlike Capote, at his death Warhol left no sense of promise unfulfilled, of a life gone awry, only of a man who knew exactly what he was doing every step of the way—except, perhaps, for the fatal last step.

Reporting the news of his death last weekend, a television anchor robot observed with all due solemnity that Warhol had moved in his career from commercial illustration to "high art." This, mind you, was said of a man noted primarily for assembly-line reproductions of soup cans, silk-screen images of movie stars, bottomlessly sloppy and self-indulgent motion pictures, and a gossip magazine for the rich and fatuous. This, in the age of Warhol, is "high art"; we utter the words with no hint of irony, no comprehension of what they say about the state to which "art" has now declined.

Only in a culture where art has lost all seriousness and standards have become meaningless could an illustrator and self-publicist such as Warhol be accepted as an artist, much less a practitioner of "high art." Yet that is how Warhol was not merely accepted but celebrated. Rather than respect him for what he was—an entertainer, a jester, of clear but decidedly limited gifts—we chose, with his own gleeful collaboration, to elevate him to what he was not: an artist.

This is to say that the words "artist" and "art" have meanings that transcend the flip usages of journalism and publicity. It is to say that art, whether it aims to exalt, to venerate, to explain or merely to amuse, is always in its innermost character serious. For centuries artists—painters, sculptors, musicians, poets—devoted their creative lives to the glory of God; later, in a more secular time, they turned to the different glories of nature and to the promise and fallibility of man. But always they were motivated by impulses that were higher than themselves, by a yearning to speak to the mysteries of the universal condition.

By such a standard how can the work of Andy Warhol

possibly be called art? Quite apart from its qualities, or lack of them, as drawing or painting, what of its inner art—its soul, if you will? What do those cans of Campbell's Soup, which Warhol happily allowed to be identified as his trademark, have to say to us? That we live in a time of mass production? Yes. That there is "art" to be found in the ordinary images of mass production? Absolutely not. This may have been Warhol's line, but the "art" itself belies the claim; it is not art at all, but illustration.

In the age of mass production, though, we have come to confuse illustration and design with art—have, in fact, rushed pell-mell to legitimize them as art. In so doing we seek to elevate them, and thus the culture to which they are so central, to heights they cannot occupy. Illustration and design are entirely authentic, useful undertakings, and it is quite possible to do them well; but no one with a reasonably mature and informed understanding of what constitutes art can be willing to accept them as anything except what they are. If reproductions of soup cans are to be given respectability as art, then so too are rock music and commercial movies and designer gowns and journalism.

Which of course is precisely what has happened. Entire industries have been created, wherever two or more illuminati have gathered, for the authentication of popular culture as "art." The distinction between what is fun and what is serious has been blurred beyond recognition, and anything goes: If it's fun, if we like it, well then it must be art. With utter solemnity, we wax rhapsodic about the "artistry" of Bob Dylan and John Lennon, about the deeper meanings in the "oeuvres" of Woody Allen and Steven Spielberg, about the "genius" of Diana Vreeland and Yves Saint Laurent, about the "literature" of Joan Didion and Hunter Thompson.

In such a culture, and in only such a culture, can the work of Andy Warhol be described as art. It is a culture, dominated by the mass media and the roaring dynamo of publicity, that rewards the immediate and superficial while having no patience with the painstaking and reflective. What matters is not whether one has anything to say, but whether one can talk—or write, or compose, or play—with the kind of facility that is easily captured by the camera or the profilist. We don't want art; we want publicity, and we have declined to such a state that we now imagine publicity to *be* art.

Warhol was an absolute master of publicity. His gift, if that is the word for it, was not for painting or film direction or magazine editing, but for self-promotion. He knew precisely how outrageous he could be and still remain within the borders of mainstream pop culture, precisely how to formulate the bon mot that would quickly pass from his lips to Johnny Carson's, precisely how to supply the raw material that feeds the voracious machinery of gossip and celebrity. He was brilliant at this and it is his achievement, albeit a most peculiar one. But he was not an artist.

Never-Never Land: II

March 9, 1987

Complete with what one television personality described as "closing ceremonies," the Goofy Games ended in Florida last week. This was the third staging of the great annual event—III Goofiad, as ABC Sports doubtless would call it—but the first to come to my attention. If it has not yet come to yours, pull up a chair; it's a story that has much to tell us about American journalism and, worse yet, American society.

The Goofy Games are staged as a publicity stunt by Disney World, which has just about cornered the market on resourceful public relations. The competitors in the "games" are not athletes but television personalities: sports reporters from a number of television stations and three-person "teams" representing their local areas. The ostensible purpose of the event is to raise money for charity—the winning team gets $10,000 for its chosen charity, and others get smaller amounts—but the real one is to drum up relatively inexpensive TV news exposure for Disney World and its manifold attractions.

Two television stations from this part of the country participated in III Goofiad: WJLA-TV in Washington and WMAR-TV in Baltimore. I watched the games on the latter, which for the moment has my fickle loyalties in the evening news competition. At Disney World's expense, the WMAR "team" and film crew went to Florida, participated in the event, and came back (as fourth-place finishers) with a $1,000 contribution toward replacing the *Pride of Baltimore*, the city's goodwill sailing ship, which sank in the Atlantic last summer; in return,

Disney World received an impressive amount of free air time on WMAR's local news, which treated the Goofy Games as a news event.

It's easy to see what Disney World gains from this lopsided quid pro quo, but rather more difficult to figure out what the television stations come away with. A spokesman at WMAR mentioned the charity, of course, and "promoting our people," by which he meant the opportunity to show his sports reporter in the Florida sun while Baltimore viewers bundle up against the late-winter chill. But the amount donated to charity is relatively small, and the promotional aspects of the event seem far less fruitful for the TV stations than for Disney World, which requires the air time as a condition of participation; had it bought the air time, according to my informant, Disney World would have paid "significantly" more than it shelled out for the WMAR team's travel expenses.

What it comes down to is that the TV stations were shilling for Disney: swapping news time in exchange for a few free trips to Florida. This is playing fast and loose with responsible journalism, but few of us in the newspaper business are in positions to moralize about it. In the past newspapers merrily swapped news space for considerations—junkets, freebies—of which readers were generally unaware, and even though many papers have cleaned up their acts the practice is still widespread. When Disney World celebrated its fifteenth anniversary a few weeks ago hundreds of editors and publishers attended at Disney's expense, and hardly a soul expressed qualms about it. Our hands, like television's, are not exactly clean.

In any event, it's not the swap of air time for a few days in Orlando that should raise our eyebrows, distasteful though it may be, but the eagerness with which we journalists collaborate in Disney's public-relations campaign. The press is full of puffery, but somehow Disney World—and, out west, Disneyland—has managed to create a special niche for itself. Disney is to PR what Barnum was to show biz: the exemplar, the guy who wrote the book. The free ink Disney gets must be measured not by the bottle but by the barrel; surely everyone else in business, industry and entertainment can only look upon its works in envy and wonder.

This kowtowing to Disney may make the press seem fairly silly, not to mention susceptible to PR manipulation, but it's worth bearing in mind that, criticism to the contrary notwithstanding, the press is fairly representative of the people who read and watch it. Disney World would not be all over the newspapers and television news shows were it not so wildly popular among people who read papers and watch television. The truly remarkable phenomenon is not Disney's public-relations triumphs, but its transformation into something approximating a national shrine.

Muslims go to Mecca, Catholics to Lourdes, Americans to Disney World. When the president of the United States wants to announce that he is not a crook, he goes to Disney World to do so; when an American reporter is released from imprisonment in Moscow, he celebrates his freedom at Disney World. If Disney would only build a hall large enough to accommodate them, the political parties no doubt would be thrilled to hold their conventions under the watchful gaze of Mickey and Minnie and Goofy. If, according to a federal judge, "secular humanism" is now a "religion," then what on earth is Disney: Santa Claus? Mom? Apple pie? Insider trading?

Whatever it is, middle-class Americans of every race, color and creed adore it. To me, this is one of life's larger mysteries. I have been to Disney World once, and each evening I kneel at my bed in fervent prayer that I shall not have to go again. But my rather violent reactions to what Walt hath wrought are not the subject of today's sermon. What matters is not that everything in Disney World is ersatz, from Mickey and Minnie to those dreadful little creatures that croon "It's a Small World," but that Americans love it so. What is it in the postwar American air that so powerfully draws us to a place that distorts, idealizes and sentimentalizes our country and ourselves? What is it about contemporary reality that has created so strong an appetite for fantasy?

The evidence of it is everywhere: at Williamsburg and Six Flags and all the other "theme parks" that in one form or another offer up the American heritage in a prettified refabrication. Like the "docudramas" that reduce important men and women from our past to made-for-television caricatures, these hugely successful tourist attractions make their money off what gives every appearance of being a national longing for oversimplification and fanciful reinvention of the real world.

The phenomenon is far easier to observe than to explain. Unlike the "social critics" who now abound on the campuses, I have no facile explanations for American popular culture, no theories about American greed and imperialism, no conviction that it's all Ronald Reagan's fault. It is one thing to see that Disney World is an American institution, quite another to figure out why. It's just there: incontrovertible and mysterious and, well, goofy.

Sex for Sale

April 13, 1987

The age of vulgarity and exploitation continues apace. Those who believe that the recent wave of political conservatism has been accompanied by a reaction against certain excesses of the sixties and seventies are advised to consider the evidence. Herewith a random sampling of life in these United States, collected last week over a period of four days:

• Jessica Hahn, the Lorelei of the fundamentalist right, was reported by *Newsweek* magazine to have given additional details of her tryst with the charismatic Jim Bakker in a tape-recorded interview. Her "sexual encounter" with Bakker in 1981 went on for "what seemed like an hour and a half," Hahn said. "I tried to get him off me," she added. "He couldn't do enough. He had to find new things to do." These "things" included intercourse and oral sex, and were followed by involuntary sexual activity with another male member of the Bakker entourage.

• *The New York Times Magazine* published an advertisement for Revlon depicting four unclothed women locked in tight embrace. The left breast of one of them—identified in the copy as Kim Alexis of Florida—was covered by a woman's hand. Whether the hand was her own or that of the model behind her—Clare Hoak of New York—apparently was for interested readers to determine. A comparison of nail-polish colors suggested the hand belonged to Kim, but the lusty look on Kim's face suggested the hand belonged to . . . Clare?

• A reader of the *Washington Post,* Sue Huff, complained in its letters column about an advertisement for Holiday Spas, published in the paper's "TV Week" section, that "features an attractive young woman wearing a bikini and posing suggestively—the sort of pose that is popular in *Playboy.*" Huff wrote: "There doesn't seem to be any excuse for this sort of sexually explicit advertising in a family magazine, especially in the one part of the newspaper that every kid looks at."

• A Washington businesswoman, Molly Peter, and a *Washington Post* writer, Margaret Engel, noted in the paper's "Outlook" section that notwithstanding a quarter century of the feminist movement, the merchandising of items that "demean women and their bodies" continues to be widespread. They made note of a catalogue from which one may order the "sexy apron," which "resembles a woman's torso and includes round removable potholders shaped like breasts," or an auto trash bag that looks like "women's black underpants," or a "conservative navy blue tie whose lining reveals a silk-screened photograph of a nude woman."

• *Manhattan, inc.,* the journal of the New York money and power crowd, published an advertisement for a health club called Definitions, which claims to offer "one-on-one personal fitness." It depicted a trimly enviable human form wearing a thin, tight gym shirt; the headline underneath read, THE ONLY SERVICE MORE PERSONALIZED THAN OURS IS ILLEGAL. The only difference between this and most other sexually exploitive advertising was that the body in question happened to be that of a man.

• The *New York Times* reported that "sex, long a prime target for television's censors, has been gaining prime-time exposure this season." This "increased frankness about sexual topics" is attributed to a number of causes, among them competition from cable television and video cassettes, "which have traditionally been more explicit than the networks," and the "economic cutbacks at the networks," which have eliminated the jobs of many in the "broadcast-standards departments," where the censoring is done. The writer-director of *Daddy*, which was shown on ABC last week, told the *Times* that teenagers on the program talk "about abortion, about condoms and diaphragms, about orgasm and ejaculation."

So there you have it: six examples—there could as well be six hundred, or six thousand—of the degree to which explicit depiction or discussion of sexual activity has become the daily staple of American life. Not a single one of these examples came from the fringes of American culture; instead they were published or broadcast in mainstream institutions of the national media, and either reported about or directed to the middle class. Not merely that, but in each instance they involved, in one measure or another, the exploitation of sexual curiosity and appetites. This was no "liberated" sexuality at work, freeing a grateful nation from the "puritanical" constraints of the past; this was, in one form or another, commerce pure and simple.

Sex has gone public to an extent that would have been inconceivable a quarter century ago, with results that can only be guessed at but that are most unlikely to be salubrious. The problem is not that we are more candid about sexuality, but that we have acquiesced in its appropriation for profit within the legitimate, as opposed to the illicit, marketplace. Yes, sex has been used to sell for years, as anyone who recalls the pin-up calendars of a half century ago well knows. But nothing in the past was even remotely comparable to what we have now: a culture in which it is commonly assumed that there are no boundaries—or that such boundaries as still remain exist primarily to be "stretched," as the panjandri of pop culture would have it.

We are to understand that this is good for us. "Some of the information may make some viewers uncomfortable," the writer-director of *Daddy* told the *Times*. "But the question we asked ourselves was whether the magnitude of the problem warranted going a little further than other shows. For us the answer was yes." This is what they all say, and what it boils down to is that the existence of a real or imagined social problem—in this case, teenage pregnancy—becomes an excuse for a sexually explicit show or article. Yes, no doubt there are well-meaning people in television and journalism who really do believe that the proliferation of explicit material will help draw attention to, and thus solve, every problem from teenage pregnancy to AIDS; but it is difficult to escape the conclusion that the motives behind much of what we watch and read have far less to do with the public weal than with rank sensationalism and private gain.

Perhaps it is priggish to say this, but I think not. To be open and adult about sexuality is one thing, and to exploit sexuality for commercial reasons is quite another. The truth is that the so-called sexual revolution produced far less genuine candor and openness than we like to think it did; as the sniggering, leering character of so much of what we watch and read suggests, we are still sexually repressed and unconfident. Rather, what the revolution did was to give license to the exploiters; and the miasma of cynical explictness in which we are engulfed leaves no doubt that they have taken that license for all it's worth.

In Thoreau's Footsteps

April 27, 1987

Back in the good old days, when eager young rubes were descending upon the great metropolises in search of fame and fortune, it used to be said that you could take the boy out of the country but you couldn't take the country out of the boy. This maxim quickly acquired the stature of universal truth. But times change, and mankind grows ever more vulgar, and maxims must alter in order to accommodate altered realities. So now the day has come to propound a new one: You can take the boy out of the city but you can't take the city out of the boy.

This profundity is inspired by a report, published last week in *The New York Times Magazine,* that for the wealthy in New York and other cities, owning a second house in the country has become a "magnificent obsession." Yes, "magnificent obsession." The story, by one Erica Abeel, went on at extravagent and ecstatic length about how in "pursuit of happiness" members of the middle- and upper-middle classes are investing in country houses for weekend and vacation use.

Abeel called the country house an "obsession," and listed it among the fads and fashions by which the age is distinguished. Not surprisingly, considering the magazine in which her article was published, it was to New York and its environs that Abeel turned her attention. With vastly less irony than her subject would seem to cry for, and with not a scintilla of indignation, Abeel documented the trend among New York's privileged not-so-few to purchase country retreats so as to shelter income from taxes, revel in "the joys of nature," flee "the city disease," and display, as conspicuously as possible, their status.

The article was, as such exercises in pop sociology so often are, a curious blend of the critical and the celebrative. Quoting the usual high priests of our unhappy age—a "distinguished psychologist," a "social commentator," a "social critic," a "cultural historian," a "sociologist," an "environmental researcher"—Abeel drew a portrait of homebuyers whose impulses have less to do with relaxation and escape than with fashion and display; these give every impression of being people desperately trying to keep pace with the pack and to flaunt their own superiority.

At the same time, though, the article—not to mention the manner in which it was presented and illustrated—was a fawning tribute to this new trend in lavish self-indulgence. With utter solemnity Abeel quoted a psychologist who addressed himself to the question of the country house and said, also with utter solemnity, that people who want to live the "good life" can't get along without a house in the country; in his view apparently, the country house is now as necessary to living well as indoor plumbing was only a couple of generations ago.

Thus it is that the country retreat has acquired not merely with-it status, but the imprimatur of the *New York Times* and a gaggle of persons represented as authorities on matters social. But a country house is not exactly a Cuisinart or a Ralph Lauren shirt or even a BMW. A country house, especially in "the environs of New York," involves the expenditure of sums calculated to stun—if not infuriate—ordinary Americans struggling to cope with a single mortgage. Though Abeel for the most part discreetly skirted the nasty matter of money—did not, in fact, mention a single real-estate price, an astonishing omission in an article devoted to expensive houses—one need only look elsewhere in the same magazine to get a sense of the kind of game being played.

There, under "Luxury Homes and Estates," are listed

houses of the sort to which weary New Yorkers flee when the

pressures of Manhattan life become oh so oppressive. A "unique and exclusive lakefront estate" in New Jersey: $1.245 million. A "spacious home" in the Catskills: $235,000. Two hundred feet of "bulkheaded ocean frontage" in Southampton: $1.1 million. A "Pocono mountain retreat": "$1 million + value; offered for immediate sale at $650,000 cash!" A "13 private acre estate" in Connecticut: $3.5 million. An "oceanfront Southern colonial" on Long Island: $10.25 million.

That, as any regular reader of "Luxury Homes and Estates" is well aware, is a mere sampling of the goodies offered to the acquisitive not-so-few through this highly popular (and, in the provinces, much-imitated) *Times Magazine* feature. The cost of showing off has gone through the roof. A $35,000 BMW just won't do it anymore; in order to express one's vulgarity to the full, it is now necessary to fork over a million or more, for which you get a house reachable only after four hours of agonizing, bumper-to-bumper driving—a house in which you live no more than forty-eight hours a week, if that.

But once you get there, according to the prevailing fiction, you are in heaven; you shed your cares as you ramble through the countryside, plucking daisies and crooning softly about the glories of Mother Nature, and the brittle veneer of the city slips away as you chew the fat with the local rustics around the cracker barrel at the gen'l store. You may walk, as Abeel suggests, in the footsteps of Henry David Thoreau, like a fellow whom she describes ambling through the woods with his daughter while preaching to her about the beauties of nature in language that would leave poor Thoreau speechless—though not, to be sure, with envy.

More likely, though, you'll just be your same old New York self. One of the unalterable truths of American life is that when New York leaves New York, New York remains resolutely . . . New York. The New York personality, forged to cope with the exigencies of life in that peculiar city, is pushy and abrasive and aggressive and, when encountered *in situ*, not without a certain charm. But the same personality when met in the bowers of Connecticut or New Jersey leaves, shall we say, something to be desired.

If anything, the words "New York" and "country" are mutually exclusive and oxymoronic. New Yorkers understand country approximately as well as country understands New York, which is to say not at all; the difference is that New York is convinced not merely that it understands country, but that it knows more about country than country itself will ever know. Thus we have the ludicrous spectacle of motor-mouthed Manhattanites speeding to the sticks in their BMWs, decking themselves out in Laurenesque parodies of rustic garb, and hunkerin' down to the pea patch. It's the ultimate Hick Chic fantasy, and fantasy is all it can ever be.

Which reminds me of my favorite New York story. Years ago I drove a cherished Manhattan friend between the North Carolina cities of Greensboro and Chapel Hill. En route we passed a sign that read: DURHAM 27, OXFORD 51. My friend turned and asked: "Is that Oxford, Mississippi?"

Sad Hearts at the Shopping Center

July 6, 1987

The tide of sin just keeps sweeping across the nation. As a result of measures that took effect last week, it is now legal to purchase a mixed drink at a public establishment in Kansas and to go shopping in Maryland on Sunday. What on earth is the country coming to?

Ruin and damnation, is what I say. If you can get a mixed drink in Kansas, next thing you know you'll be able to dance in the aisle of the First Baptist Church or sing "Why Don't We Do It in the Road?" in Tipper Gore's breakfast nook. As for Sunday shopping in Maryland, why, that stretches the imagination just about as far as it can go, and then some. Imagine! The very idea!

There's no getting around it: Sin has come to Maryland in all its fury, and by the end of the week the citizens of that once proud state will be wallowing in it: Packing the family into the wagon and blissing out at K mart, letting the kids go wild in Toys "R" Us, getting down and dirty at Banana Republic, blowing the budget at Brookstone, wallowing in conspicuous display at Saks Fifth Avenue: Have they no principles? Have they no morals? Have they no shame?

More to the point: Have they no sense? The pertinent question is not whether people should be allowed to shop on Sunday but why on earth they would want to—on Sunday or, for that matter, any other day of the week. Doesn't anyone out there understand that the great era of American shopping is over, kaput, sayonara? Shopping in America is now approximately as much fun as mowing the lawn or washing the dishes: It's the same old shtick, over and over and over.

Years from now, when the grandchildren gather around their grandpappy's knee, I'll lean back, put a reminiscent smile on my face, and mistily reflect: "You kids were just born too late. Why, back when I was a pup a man was a man and a shop was a shop. You could go into a store and see something there you couldn't see anywhere else. Shopping was an adventure then, kids, for the bold and the determined. Why, now shopping's so boring and so easy, just about anybody can do it."

And just about everybody does. They talk about "recreational shopping" as the national pastime, or the national disease, but what I want to know is: What's so recreational about it? What fun's to be had when every mall not merely looks precisely like the last mall, but has precisely the same shops? It's the ultimate time warp. Whether you're in Stamford or Minneapolis, Baltimore or San Francisco, you find only the same damned stores selling the same damned products.

The full picture dawned on me a couple of months ago when, after flying from Baltimore to San Francisco, I decided to explore that city's downtown shopping district. I strolled along—past a Doubleday Book Store and a McDonald's and other branches and franchises of national enterprises—when suddenly I found myself directly in front of . . . I can barely bring myself to type the words . . . directly in front of Jos. A. Bank. I had gotten just about as far from Baltimore as one can get and still be in the continental United States, and there I was, belly to belly with Baltimore's most famous haberdasher.

Jos. A. Bank. I first heard of it about two decades ago. You could buy its clothing two ways, by visiting the store in Baltimore or by ordering through its catalogue. That was it; Joe Bank was Baltimore through and through. But now, like virtually everybody else, it's everywhere; which is to say that in terms of distinctiveness, it's nowhere. I still buy its clothes, because I like (some of) them, but somehow the thrill is gone.

Ditto with the record store down the street. When I moved to Baltimore in 1978 it was a dingy place called Record and Tape Collector. Its decor left a good deal to be desired, but its stock was ample and its staff both helpful and friendly. After dinner the beagle and I used to wander down for a browse; she'd go in one direction, looking for crumbs, and I'd go in another, looking for music. The staff welcomed both of us: The dog got friendly pats and I got a steady customer's special discount.

But now Record and Tape Collector is gone. It is called Record World, just like all the other Record Worlds that are popping forth up and down the East Coast. The floors have been carpeted and the classical LPs eliminated; at Record World—"record"?—it's compact disks or tape cassettes or else. The tapes are behind glass doors; if you want to look at one a salesperson unlocks the doors and stands by, presumably on shoplifter alert. The salespeople seem friendly, but all my old friends are gone, and I could no more take the beagle there than I could take her to Brooks Brothers.

Speaking of which. When I was a pup and my pappy was fixin' me in WASPish ways, a trip to Brooks—"Mr. Brooks," my father called him, or it, or them—was an event of religious significance. There were only two Brooks stores then, one downtown and the other midtown, and to pass through the heavy doors that opened onto Madison Avenue was to pass into Westminister Abbey. But now Brooks is everywhere, just like the pro sports leagues. It's even in Miami; Brooks Brothers in Miami—the ultimate oxymoron. Soon it will be in Baltimore, right there at the Inner Harbor with all the other branches and franchises. I rather doubt that as I pass through these doors I will feel myself to be entering upon a religious experience.

Clothes may or may not make the man, or the woman, but they do a lot less making when they are the same clothes that everyone else is wearing. To all intents and purposes distinctivness has vanished from the American marketplace, except in a few of the shops that cater to the very rich and the artsy-craftsy places that deal in "folk" creations. To wear a shirt that displays

Brooks Brothers' golden fleece or Ralph Lauren's polo player is not to express one's distinctiveness but to participate in an advertising campaign.

That people should want to spend their Sundays in stores selling these products, when they could be eating hard-shell crabs or sailing on the Chesapeake, is quite beyond me, but the one absolute certainty is that they will. An employee of a major mall outside Baltimore said last week that Sunday shopping will have a significant effect on business there, and no doubt she was right. Quite apart from the convenience that Sunday shopping offers to people who are preoccupied during the week with households and jobs, the lure of the mall is simply more than most Americans resist; another day in which to succumb to it can only be heaven.

But if people are going to spend Sundays in mall heaven, they ought to do themselves a favor and have a bit of fun while they're at it. One of the truly perplexing oddities of American life is that so few of these people doing "recreational shopping" seem to be enjoying themselves. You'll find as many glum faces in a mall today as you found in Sunday school a century ago. Maybe that's the point: In church or at the mall, on Sunday we pay for our sins. But now we use credit cards.

"Character" in Washington

September 21, 1987

How sweetly ironic it is that in political Washington, where character counts for approximately as much as taste does in Hollywood, "character" is now the fashion of the day. Gary Hart has departed the presidential wars, his "character" called into question; Joseph Biden teeters on the edge of elimination, his "character" now seen as insufficient; Robert Bork's nomination to the Supreme Court hangs in the balance, his "character" the hidden issue behind the criticism of vacillation and inconsistency in his legal views.

Washington has discovered "character" much as Sutter discovered gold: eureka! From every nook and cranny the prospectors now emerge, each determined to stake his or her claim on the politically vendible product called "character." But what is most apparent is that none of them has the foggiest idea what character actually is, which is why it is necessary to put the word in quotation marks when using it as political Washington does. For what Washington regards as "character" is something quite different from character as it is commonly understood.

Like "values," "character" has become a buzzword. Ostensibly it stands for honor, conviction and probity, the qualities commonly associated with strength of character, but in actuality it means playing by the rules within the boundaries of the political field. A dalliance now and then is all right—without dalliance, Washington would be at a loss for dinner conversation—but it must be discreet and tasteful; Gary Hart's was neither, hence his dismissal. Oratorical plagiarism is all right, too—

speechwriting is not, after all, the most original or elevated of arts—but getting caught at it is not; Biden was nailed, hence his present discomfort.

It is no oversimplification to say that in Washington, and wherever else two or more politicians may gather, he who does not get caught has "character" and he who gets caught has none. Politics may be a rather amoral business but it is also a practical one, and politicians are more comfortable dealing with what one can get away with than with the moral import of one's actions. Hart's well-earned reputation as a Lothario probably won him more envy than disrepute in the political community so long as he kept his amours reasonably private; but Donna Rice was his Fannye Fox and *Monkey Business* was his Tidal Basin—it was all too blatant and too public and, like Wilbur Mills, Hart had to pay the piper.

But even when Washington finds it necessary to go off on a righteous toot, as it did with Hart and seems eager to do with Biden, it is far less concerned with the "character" of the individual involved than with the political dimensions of his actions. With Hart and Biden alike, the word that recurred over and over was "contain": Could disclosures about their behavior be "contained," or would they go out of control and alter the candidates' political prospects? The talk about "character" was strictly for public consumption; "containment," so far as political Washington is concerned, was the real issue.

This is not to say that the political community never is genuinely concerned about the "character" of public figures, only that its definition of the term is shaped not by considerations of rectitude or personality but by the prevailing political wisdom. Thus, for example, Washington's indignation over Biden's penchant for plagiarism is exceeded only by its indifference to his artificial hair and his tendency to refer to himself in public discourse in the third person. To the outside observer, Biden's inability to accept his incipient baldness might seem a sign of callowness and his talk about "Joe Biden" a sign of insuperable arrogance, but manufactured appearances and bloated egos are so common in Washington that no one took notice—even though such attributes surely do not speak well for the character of those afflicted with them.

With unerring accuracy, Washington fixes its indignation on the obvious and overlooks what is genuinely revealing. Egged on by a press blissed out on sensation, it works itself into a frenzy over the passing scandal of womanizing or plagiarism yet conveniently ignores the subtler signs suggesting, perhaps, that one official's arrogance masks a lack of self-confidence, or that another's inflated rhetoric disguises an undisciplined mind. This is not to say that womanizing and plagarism are unrevealing or unimportant—quite to the contrary—but that there were plenty of other warning signs before these were discovered, signs that Washington either failed to recognize or chose to overlook.

It may be true, to be sure, that a realistic view demands that character be defined somewhat differently within the political context than it is elsewhere. Politics is indeed the art of the possible, a reality that cannot but affect moral or personal judgments about those who participate in it. But if we accept that proposition, it leaves still unresolved the question of definition: Within the political context what can truly be called character, devoid of quotation marks?

Herewith a modest suggestion: A politician of character is one whose convictions are genuine rather than tailored to convenience, whose commitment to public service is greater than his avarice, whose word can be taken more or less at face value, whose probity is beyond dispute, and whose personal behavior falls within socially acceptable boundaries. That may be a bit wordy for Webster, but it is an effort to accommodate idealism to reality. It is too much, for example, to expect that our politicians always tell us the truth; in fact it may not always be in our best interests for them to do so. It is too much, as well, for us to expect them to maintain personal standards that we ourselves do not; a society with a higher tolerance for adultery than it may care to admit should not be overly judgmental about a politician who strays from time to time in an environment that offers considerable temptation.

Thus Franklin Roosevelt, whose liaisons with Lucy Mercer seem to have been relatively innocent and inconsequential, satisfies on all counts the definition of political character; so too does Dwight Eisenhower, whose mysterious relationship with Kaye Summersby seems to have been similarly innocuous. But John Kennedy's obsessive philandering and his irresponsible affair with Judith Campbell Exner disqualify him, as does Warren Harding's cozy relationship with the architects of Teapot Dome.

What it all boils down to is a question of honesty: Is a politician honest with his constituents and, even more important, with himself? This may seem a fairly basic standard by which to measure political character, but it is better than no standard at all, which is what political Washington now offers us. As to whether the current aspirants for the presidency meet this definition, that is a judgment each voter must draw from the evidence; but the evidence, on the whole, is not especially encouraging.

So Much for "Literature"

January 11, 1988

Just when you thought it was safe to go back to English class, here come the professors again. "Many college professors," the *New York Times* reported last week, "are re-thinking the very notion of what is literature." A "rising group" among the professoriat "contends the idea of an enduring pantheon of writers and their works is an elitist one largely defined by white men who are Northeastern academics and critics."

According to these vigilantes of the English departments, literary quality is irrelevant; they believe in "the teaching of writers principally for historical and sociological importance, for what they have to say rather than how well they say it." Thus "choosing between Virginia Woolf and Pearl Buck, they hold, involves political and cultural distinctions more than aesthetic ones." According to a professor at the University of Pennsylvania named Houston Baker—take down that name, officer—"It's no different from choosing between a hoagy and a pizza. I am one whose career is dedicated to the day when we have a disappearance of those standards."

Makes you want to rush right back to college, doesn't it? To hell with Shakespeare and Milton, Emerson and Faulkner! Let's boogie! Let's take courses in the writers who really matter, the writers whom the WASPish old guard sneers at. Let's get relevant, with courses on Gothic novels, bodice-ripper romances, Westerns, detective stories—all of which, the *Times* advises us, "are proliferating" in the English departments.

The reason they are proliferating, the new professoriat

would have us believe, is that they bring elements into the literary "canon" that had previously been excluded from it. Quite specifically, they say that blacks and women have been excluded. In so saying they conveniently ignore the high place long accorded such black writers as W.E.B. DuBois, Richard Wright, Langston Hughes, James Baldwin, Ralph Ellison and Jean Toomer, not to mention such women writers as Emily Dickinson, Amy Lowell, Edith Wharton, Willa Cather, Flannery O'-Connor, Eudora Welty and Marianne Moore—but who cares about the facts when the real game being played has nothing to do with literature and everything to do with retrograde sixties politics and academic careerism?

What the professors decline to tell us, as they rush pell-mell to ditch Faulkner and sanctify Louis L' Amour, is that they are busily at work on their own hidden agenda, the first part of which involves institutionalizing the political sentiments that were prevalent on the campuses two decades ago. Though most people who went through college in those days eventually grew up and entered the real world, others stayed in school and made places for themselves in the professioral bureaucracy—especially in the humanities departments, which since the sixties have had little to offer their graduate students by way of career opportunities except appointments (and precious few of them) in the humanities departments. They clung tenaciously to their politics, with its sentimental prattle about the "worker-student alliance," its patronization of blacks and its strident feminism, and they encouraged each other in the conviction that it is the only good and true politics.

In time, of course, the professoriat being such as it is, they got tenure and rose to positions of prominence in that most ludicrous of American institutions, the Modern Language Association. Now, from this vantage point of what passes for power in their little world, they are steadfastly establishing the new order of things, the essence of which is that literature as previously we knew it no longer matters. Political orthodoxy matters.

Or, as the *Times* more politely puts it: "Once-honored standards like grace of style, vigor of prose and originality of expression have been downgraded or questioned while the importance of historical and social impact and rhetorical strength has grown."

All of which may sound high-minded to some ears, but it disguises the rather less noble motive that is the other part of these young fascists' agenda. A central fact of life in the humanities departments, the English departments in particular, is that all the really good subjects for study already have been taken—have, in fact, been studied right into the ground. If there is anything left to be said about Hawthorne or Hemingway, Melville or Crane, Longfellow or Frost, it could only be said by a person of such originality of mind as to border on genius, and there are approximately as many such people in the English department bureaucracy as there are in your average insurance-company bureaucracy.

No, the English departments are populated by ordinary people of ordinary abilities whose chief aim in life is to secure position and tenure for themselves. With the good subjects for study already taken, they have done the perfectly sensible thing and invented new subjects around which to construct their careers. This means that they must invest those subjects with academic legitimacy: hence the rush to cover with glory writers and books that previously had been properly regarded as of minor stature and therefore of minor scholarly interest. If you can make a case for Zora Neale Hurston or Edith Summers Kelley as a writer of consequence, then similarly you can make a case for a career based on the study of that writer of consequence.

In the process you can take a few well-aimed swipes at what remains of the academic and critical establishment, which at some institutions still has an anachronistically WASPish coloration. It is historical fact that some members of this establishment reacted with horror and outrage to the excesses of the sixties, as well they should have, and that in some instances they allowed their own political and social views to affect tenure decisions involving younger faculty, as well they should not have. The result has been a lot of intergenerational tension in the humanities departments—giving them, in this if nothing else, something in common with the real world—and a great opportunity for the young turks to get back at their "oppressors" as the passage of time forces the changes in departmental personnel that the old men resisted.

All of which is to say that there is a lot more to the "rethinking of literature" than the new humanities establishment is willing to admit. In fact it is no exaggeration to say that literature itself is not an issue here at all, for these people simply do not understand or care about literature as the term traditionally has been understood. Not merely are they careerists and political schemers, they are also children of the age of semiotics and deconstruction, an age in which it is taught in the English departments that the critic is more important than the artist and that the interpretation is more important than the work. This is balderdash to the core, but then so too, these days, are the English departments.

The Fun Ethic

June 13, 1988

If you're an ambitious young person who'd like a career in academic life but fears that all of the most interesting scholarly departments already are overpopulated, fear not. A whole new academic discipline has been invented; it is growing so rapidly that 1,740 people gave speeches at its recent convention in New Orleans, and—here is the best part of all—it's *fun:* as much fun as rock 'n' roll music, kung-fu movies and Final Four basketball games.

They call it popular culture, with capital letters. The Popular Culture Association met in New Orleans not long ago, and a reporter from the *Wall Street Journal* was on hand to assess the proceedings. His dispatch appeared in that newspaper last week; a depressing document it most certainly is—still further evidence that American higher education, in lockstep with the larger national culture, is marching into the fairyland of entertainment and escape.

The guru of popular culture, the *Journal* discovered, is Ray Browne, "a peppery sixty-six-year-old professor and academic entrepreneur who has singlehandedly turned Ohio's Bowling Green State University into the Lourdes of popular culture." When first Browne started teaching the subject, about two decades ago, "I was like Socrates, if you'll pardon the allusion. I was misspending state money, embarrassing the university and corrupting the youth." But now Bowling Green so loves popular culture that it is looking into the authorization of a Ph.D. program in the subject, which if approved should go a long way toward putting Bowling Green on the academic map—which, in case you hadn't figured it out already, is precisely what academic entrepreneurship is all about.

"More and more people are discovering they really are bored in academia," Browne says. "They don't have any fun." So popular culture has come to the rescue: "This is a rejuvenation. It's an intellectual fat farm." You can say that again: it's a farm for reducing intellectual inquiry to inadvertent self-parody, as an examination of the proceedings in New Orleans all too abundantly demonstrates.

The meeting of the Popular Culture Association lasted four days and included, as previously noted, no fewer than 1,740 speeches—or, as they are called at academic gatherings, papers. One of these, presented by a teacher of communications at Bradley University in Illinois, was called—are you ready for this?—"The Reconciliation of Archie and Meathead: 'All in the Family's' Last Episode." Another, entitled "Body Slam: Professional Wrestling as Greek Drama," included the following pithy observation:

"The first step toward a just appreciation of wrestling involves a return to an aesthetics that discards modern notions of authenticity or truth and embraces notions of mimesis that are more in line with those of a Johnson or an Aristotle."

There's more, folks. Other papers the *Journal* tracked down include: "Opium, Coleridge and the Beatles," "Marketing Odor: A Historical Analysis of Perfume Ads in Selected Magazines," "The Final Four as Final Judgment: The NCAA Basketball Tournament," "Yogi Berra: The Dumb Philosopher?" and "The American Garage Sale and Its Cultural Implications."

Is it to laugh, or to weep? The answer, I fear, is the latter. Heaven knows it is easy enough to make sport of the ladies and gentlemen of popular culture, with their seminars on cookbooks and comic strips, their solemn rhetoric about "contemporary archaeology," their twaddle about the "aesthetic value" of—no kidding—Joan Rivers, except that what they are doing is all too symptomatic of recent developments in academic life particularly and the country generally. The work ethic is but a memory; it's the fun ethic that now drives us.

The rise of popular culture as an academic "discipline" merely reflects the rise of similarly frivolous pursuits elsewhere on campus. The "study" of sport, previously limited to the physical-education departments, now has moved into the schools of literature and history and sociology, as members of the professoriat—and their all-too-willing students—fabricate elaborate academic legitimizations for what used to be called plain old jock sniffing. In the English departments, whole courses are now devoted to Westerns—there is actually a course at Duke University, which once knew better, called "Home on the Range: The Western in American Culture"—and mysteries and contemporary popular fiction.

Various rationales are offered for including these "courses" in what are alleged to be scholarly curricula, but what they all boil down to is that studying the Beatles and Jacqueline Susann and John Wayne is a lot easier, and a lot more fun, than studying Bach and Faulkner and Ibsen. "Popular culture" is not an academic course but a form of escape: from the obligation to ground oneself in the rich, complex intellectual legacy of the past, and from the not inconsiderable difficulties of self-discipline. Whether it is a course in Westerns as "literature" or one in the aesthetics of professional wrestling, it has nothing to do with scholarship and everything to do with self-indulgence.

But if this trend toward trivialization is especially evident and lamentable in the universities, it scarcely is unique to them. Now that we are well into the age of television and mass communications, we have accommodated ourselves to the realities of that age and have become an entertainment culture. What we seek above all else is not knowledge or understanding but amusement; our children cannot locate France or Massachusetts on maps and cannot answer simple mathematical questions on routine tests, but they are richly versed—with the complicity of the professoriat—in the oeuvre of Pink Floyd and the witticisms of Lawrence Peter "Yogi" Berra.

Obviously this is not a universal phenomenon; serious work is still being done by serious people on the campuses, just as such work is being done by such people elsewhere in the society. An entire school of arts and sciences cannot be dismissed out of hand because of a single course on Louis L'Amour, and it is not my intention to do so. But it is disturbing all the same to see the universities knuckling under to lazy professors and lazy students, permitting the standards of academic life to be undermined by people whose interests lie not in genuine scholarship but in careerism and self-indulgence.

It is from such motives, no doubt about it, that the "popular culture" movement sprang. It stands now as a monument, one that seems fated in today's permissive climate to grow ever larger, to the standards of the fun ethic. Anyone who seeks to pass it off as an academic discipline is either self-deluded or a fool.

The Age of Psychology

July 4, 1988

The news will scarcely be surprising to anyone who keeps an eye on the workings of American justice, but it was reported last week that "professional clinicians do not in fact make more accurate clinical judgments than laypersons" about the insanity or propensity to violence of criminal suspects. Or, to put it another way: A court is as likely to get an intelligent surmise about human behavior from an insurance salesman or a truck driver as it is from a psychiatrist or a psychologist—more likely, perhaps, since the former may well have broader knowledge of actual, real-world human behavior than the latter.

The report in *Science* magazine cannot be dismissed by the community of latter-day phrenologists as the work of ignorant outsiders for it comes from within that community; both of its authors are psychologists, one a director of a hospital in Rhode Island and the other an attorney specializing in expert witnesses. They studied fourteen hundred cases in which the judgments of psychiatrists and psychologists were employed by the courts, and concluded that "clinicians are wrong at least twice as often as they are correct." In both prediction and diagnosis, they found, clinicians and laymen are equally expert—or, more accurately, equally inexpert. In certain circumstances, they wrote, a secretary is as reliable a judge of brain damage as a psychologist.

No doubt this report will be cited, as well it should be, as further evidence against the wholesale use of psychological testimony in court, but its implications are considerably broader than that. Many labels can be and have been applied to the age in which we live, but the Age of Psychology surely must be among the most accurate and telling. In our country of the blindly narcissistic, the one-eyed psychologist is king: an omnipresent demigod whose judgments, however misguided or even lunatic they may be, we seek as messages from Delphi.

Thus it is that in the courts the testimony of psychologists and psychiatrists—testimony fundamentally speculative by nature—is employed as routinely as that of police officers and private eyes, often at exorbitant fees. As the astonishing trial of John Hinckley, Jr., revealed, this testimony can take whatever direction a psychologist and his employer of the moment wish it to, with the result that a courtroom can quickly become overrun with statements about a defendant's mental condition and motives that have nothing in common except that they are delivered by "experts," some of whom make their careers out of issuing pronunciamentos in court.

It's a transparently cynical business, one that does a good deal more for the wallets of the psychologists than for defendants and plaintiffs or for the orderly, equitable operation of the law. Yet we cling resolutely to it, out of the persistent belief that somehow the heirs of Doktor Freud have been granted exclusive access to the most mysterious recesses of the human mind and psyche. Is there anything in which the age has greater faith than the divining powers of anyone who has spent a few years in one school or another and emerged with a piece of paper declaring him or her qualified to dissect human souls?

Never mind that in truth this person is scarcely more competent than you or I to formulate such dicta; what matters is that some university has authenticated his powers, so therefore they must be infallible. Thus it is that whenever we gentlemen and ladies of the news media find ourselves confronted with what we take to be an event of major significance, to whom do we turn to interpret it? Our favorite tea leaf readers, of course: the psychologists. A spell of hot weather, an airplane crash, the Super Bowl, a stock-market slide, the Christmas holidays: To explain the mysteries of these and all other great occasions, we have at our beck and call an army—nay, a veritable host—of experts positively bristling with doktorates.

Therefore the feature writer, assigned a "mood of the holidays" report, can turn with confidence to a psychologist at any local hospital or university for instant expertise. Emitting great bursts of flatulent psychobabble, this eminence will pronounce: "In times of communal celebration and ritual, our unconscious memory recalls the gratifications of childhood and we seek to recapture them through duplicative behavior that reinforces our sense of self and our membership in the larger tribe." Or: at New Year's we drink too much and at Christmas we want presents.

Psychobabble is everywhere: the noise of the age. Were there no psychobabble and no psychologists to spout it, Phil Donahue and Oprah Winfrey would go out of business overnight, a socially desirable prospect but one most unlikely to materialize so long as we thirst to find the keys to our innermost secrets. Local television newscasts—national ones too, for that matter—would have to shut down were they to be deprived of their five-second spots of instant, in-depth analysis that "tell it like it is" in the darkest reaches of the soul.

Even in literature, where one might think people would know better, psychology holds sway. Biographers, few if any of whom are licensed to form psychiatric judgments, routinely bring their distinctly amateur talents to bear on the minds and psyches of their subjects; some put common sense to use and interpret the lives at hand with subtlety and discretion, but others rush in where even Freud himself probably would have feared to tread. In fiction the psychiatrist is an increasingly familiar presence, pronouncing judgments about characters' lives and motives that authors are too lazy or uninventive to reach through the more difficult means of characterization and story.

As to pop psychology, there is scarcely any need to elaborate upon its ubiquity. From the television talk shows to the best-seller list, vendors of facile counsel about matters psychological are as plentiful as the flowers that bloom in the spring. Their advice is approximately as reliable as that to be found in the astrological tables or a box of fortune cookies, but we cannot have enough of it, and in the process we make millionaires out of an endless succession of charlatans, poseurs, snake-oil salesmen and mountebanks.

The pity of it is that in the process we lose sight of the one area in which psychologists—some of them, at least—have a legitimate and valuable contribution to make. Practiced in responsible hands, psychiatric and/or psychological therapy can have salubrious effects for troubled individuals and families. Though it's probably true that a certificate of alleged competence in psychology is less important to effective therapy than a willing ear, a good heart and a wealth of experience in life, it is also true that too much good has been done in psychological therapy to dismiss it along with all the psychological prattle that fills the public air.

But this prattle seems to be what we most want, and what too many publicity-seeking shrinks are most eager to give us. Whether in the courtroom or over the airwaves, in the bookstores or the press, we are afflicted with a plague of psychobabble. We imagine it to be the message from the oracle, but it's really only noise.

"Eurocentrism"

April 17, 1989

There's a new buzzword in education, and like many such words it's a mouthful: Eurocentrism. It refers, rarely in a positive sense, to an American culture that is obsessed with its Western, or European, heritage and is largely oblivious to the history and influence of the rest of the world. To those who use the word to attack American culture and education, Eurocentrism is provincial at best and racist at worst; but however one defines it, Eurocentrism has divided educators in an unpleasantly virulent controversy.

It originated, as such matters often do, in the colleges and universities, where in recent years there has been powerful pressure from a number of groups—women, racial and ethnic minorities, station-wagon Marxists—who believe that history, literature and other subjects are taught with a bias that is white, male and European. These groups contend—rightly, as it happens—that there is more to history and literature than such a bias admits, and that in order to correct it curricula must be revised so as to be more widely inclusive.

It was in this climate that the celebrated, or notorious, restructuring of Stanford University's undergraduate requirements was conducted. Whether Stanford responded positively to a legitimate grievance or merely caved in to the protests of noisy and well-organized malcontents is still a matter of debate, but it remains that Stanford students are now required to read the work of some writers who are chosen as much for their sex or race as for the actual quality of their work.

Now the trickle-down effect is being felt lower in the educational system. California has established what seems to be a sensible and thoughtful history curriculum for the public schools, in which students will be expected not merely to study the history of Asia and Africa but also—*mirabile dictu!*—to devote many more classroom hours to history of all kinds than they now do. If this reform produces students who are more educated about the past and its lessons than the present system does, it will be one of the miracles of the age.

But if California's reform is successful, in large measure it will be because the state seems to have made a real effort to insulate the process of revision from excessive influence by persons and groups whose interests are more political than educational. A primary architect of the new curriculum was Diane Ravitch, of Columbia University, who brought to the task the same balance of cultural conservatism and sensitivity to social diversity with which she has addressed other educational issues; she and her colleagues were properly alert to legitimate complaints about Eurocentrism, but they also declined to diminish emphasis on "Europe as the seedbed of democratic institutions," as Ravitch told the *New York Times* last week.

In the same story in which Ravitch was quoted, there was an instructive example of the political interests that are being brought to bear in the debate over Eurocentrism. According to Molefi Asante, who is the chairman of African-American Studies at Temple University, "We are not living in a Western country. The American project is not yet completed. It is only in the eyes of the Eurocentrists who see it as a Western project, which means to hell with the rest of the people who have yet to create the project." What is needed, according to Asante, is an "Afrocentric and Latinocentric" view of the world.

This hardly bodes well for the public schools of Camden, a depressed and ravaged city in New Jersey the public-school curriculum of which Asante has been charged with rewriting. If he practices what he preaches, it seems likely that the schoolchildren of Camden—most of whom already have entered the world at a crippling disadvantage—will be educated in ways that can do little to help them find productive and satisfying careers for themselves in a society that, for all its ethnic, racial and cultural diversity, remains deeply Western both in history and outlook.

America was first settled by Europeans who established governmental institutions based on Western models and created a social order founded in Western precepts. In the ensuing centuries this society absorbed people from other cultures to an astonishing extent, and it absorbed their cultures along with them; one need only eat American food, listen to American music or read American prose to appreciate the extent to which this culture's Western character has been shaped by decidedly non-Western influences.

Yet its essential character is as a Western as ever. If the United States absorbs other people and their cultures, it also expects them to absorb, and conform to, its own. On the most obvious level, this means that we expect them to speak the country's Western language and obey its Western laws. It also means that we expect them to accept certain assumptions involving individual rights, the value of human life and other philosophical matters to which the West has addressed itself over the centuries.

It does not mean, or certainly should not, that we expect them to abandon or denigrate their histories. It does us no credit that for generations we have assumed that the only history worth knowing apart from our own is that of England and the Continent. Not merely is this an indefensible slur on people of different backgrounds, but it is simply bad history, a reflection of our ignorance about the rest of the world and our persistent refusal to take its past seriously.

To whatever extent the opponents of Eurocentrism may force us to teach history in a multicultural context and to read literature similarly, their efforts will be valuable and welcome. There is reason to believe, though, that many of those who cry so loudly about the injustice of Eurocentrism have nothing more elevated in mind than replacing one form of cultural, ethnic and racial narrowmindedness with another. Precisely how an "Afrocentric and Latinocentric" approach to history would improve upon a Eurocentric one is anything except clear; but it looks for all the world as if proponents of this scheme were less interested in genuine justice than in achieving primacy for another form of racism, one that merely happens to be their own.

This certainly would be change, but it scarcely would be progress. The truth is that, though few of those moaning about Eurocentrism would admit it, a principal theme in the history of the United States is the gradual blurring of ethnic, racial and cultural distinctions into a national character that may be predominantly Western but is most accurately called American. We may retain some of those distinctions as we enter the American mix, but it is the mix that matters most—and it is this that those who insist on "centrism" of any kind seek to repudiate.

Let's All Have a Good Cry

August 14, 1989

The closing item on NBC's evening news broadcast last Thursday was about Dave Dravecky, a pitcher for the San Francisco Giants who had, that very afternoon, concluded a dramatic and improbable recovery from major surgery. Nearly a year ago a malignant tumor had been removed from Dravecky's pitching arm, and doctors had told him that his career in the majors was over; yet here he was, on a fine California afternoon, celebrating his return from the abyss by allowing only three runs in eight innings and earning an important victory for his ball club.

The Dravecky story faded away and the camera returned to Tom Brokaw, the anchorman, who gave the audience an avuncular nod—the gesture seems to be his equivalent of Dan Rather's pullover sweater—and said, as he closed the show, that he *loved* that kind of story. Don't we all? Riches to rags to riches: A person in the middle of a successful career is cruelly and randomly struck down, yet refuses to give in, fights back with determination and faith, and in the end returns, if only for an afternoon, to his former glory—it's sob-sister material of the ripest variety, and who among us can resist it?

But has anyone out there noticed that sob journalism of one sort or another has become so prevalent and virulent that we're in danger of being overrun by it? Not merely in the supermarket tabloid magazines and the late-afternoon talk shows but also in the network news and the most respectable newspapers and magazines, "human interest" stories are everywhere. A great outpouring of sentiment is upon us, in which we are happily wallowing when, instead, we should be considering what it says about how the media, in their insatiable need to fill time and space, are turning every aspect of our lives into entertainment.

A paraplegic scales a mountain, with cameras tracking his every movement, and ends up in the White House for a photo opportunity with the president; a journeyman minor leaguer suddenly finds himself the starring pitcher for his home-town big-league team, and the cameras are right there to record his tears of joy; men and women in various states of physical disability walk or run or pedal or propel their wheelchairs across great distances, with the media marking every milepost—on and on it goes, this procession of ordinary human beings whose struggles are seized upon by the piranhas of journalism and turned into heart wrenchers for a nation of voyeurs.

No doubt some of those on whom the cameras focus are self-promoters and publicity seekers, but most are people who happen into the limelight by pure accident yet feel duty-bound to abide by its incessant demands. Surely one of the oddest and least appealing aspects of contemporary life is the willingness—no, the eagerness—of people in extreme conditions to bare themselves for the benefit of the media. A mother whose son has just been murdered tells the story of his last minute to a reporter for the local news broadcast; a family whose house has burned to the ground meekly answers every question posed by a correspondent for the daily newspaper; a neighbor animatedly gives a blow-by-blow account of the domestic violence next door to a crowd of reporters and cameramen—one by one we line up for our turns in the spotlight, doing the bidding of the media at precisely the hour when we should seek, and be granted, privacy and peace.

That we are being exploited at every turn seems not to bother us in the least. The people who spill forth the most intimate details of their lives for Oprah and Sally and Phil and Geraldo seem utterly unaware that they are being used, seem if anything to regard it as an obligation of citizenship in this Republic of Videotape to confess their sins with alacrity and joy. Ditto for those who, before the blood has yet dried on the road, offer up their eyewitness accounts of carnage by automobile or execution by Uzi. When last did we hear someone say to a reporter or cameraman, "Leave me alone; this is none of your business; go away"? These words may be uttered by indicted coconspirators and Mafia chieftains, but not by those of us out there in the crowd, yearning for our five seconds of sound-bite fame.

So it should please us to learn that in the future the opportunities for this bizarre form of self-expression are certain to increase. The newspapers and magazines haven't much more room for sob stories—though at times they seem to be straining mightily to make more—but on television the space grows day by day. As competition becomes ever more vigorous, with the rise of cable and the proliferation of independent production companies, television is discovering that "news" is a relatively cheap, endlessly fruitful and hugely popular way both to fill empty time and to lure viewers.

Thus we have the prime-time "news" broadcasts that the networks are now trotting out and the proliferation of "magazines" the independents market to fill those vacant half-hour spots immediately before and after the prime evening hours. These programs are not devoted to anything approximating serious coverage of serious issues and/or events, but are entertainment shows posing as news. Their purpose is not to inform or enlighten but to amuse and exploit; inasmuch as (a) there are a great many of them and (b) they have a great deal of time to fill, anyone and anything are fodder for their cameras.

What they give us is a peculiar mixture of sob story and feel-good uplift. With a cynicism that would be remarkable were it not so commonplace, they track down stories of ordinary human suffering or forebearance or persistence and transform them into minidramas calculated not merely to entertain us but also to persuade us that the people broadcasting them are our friends. The station I watch most often in Baltimore bills itself as "Friends You Can Turn To," an utterly empty slogan—could I turn to them for a loan? a ride to work? a hand with the dishes?—but one that epitomizes the feel-good craze now sweeping through Medialand.

The rock upon which the fad has been constructed is, in truth, pure mush: the good old-fashioned human-interest story, modernized by the technology of television and universalized by the desire we all seem to share to be filmed by its cameras. We've been described as a nation of passive witnesses, and in a sense we certainly are, but we're also a nation of would-be participants, yearning to put our private emotions—elation or sorrow, joy or grief, it makes no difference—on public display.

In the process, though, we devalue and debase those emotions. When stories of triumph against adversity become camera fodder, as cheap as the film on which they are told, eventually they lose meaning and pertinence; each of them is just another float in the passing parade. Dave Dravecky's jubilation might have been real to him, but to us it is merely last Thursday's news, a small catch in the throat we've long since forgotten. Now we need new news, new sensation, new sentimentality: Step right up, folks, your moment in the sun is here.

The Tyranny of the New

September 11, 1989

In all the blather to which we've been subjected by the arts community on the subject of the Helms Amendment, which would place certain restrictions on federal expenditures for the arts and humanities, a recurrent theme has been that government has an obligation not merely to support art but, in particular, to support art that is controversial and "new." That this is at best a dubious proposition is self-evident, but of one thing we can be certain: It reflects assumptions about the nature and purpose of art that are utterly central to modernism.

The question of controversial art was deftly treated the other day by Jules Feiffer, who in a satirical drawing showed an artist going through a routine execrating middle-class society and government on every imaginable count, then closing with the emphatic demand: "FUND ME!" That taxpayers should be expected to subsidize artists and writers who routinely revile them is one of the age's odder hypotheses, but the artistic and literary communities regard it as holy writ; implicit in it is the supposition, preposterous on its face, that controversy is in and of itself desirable.

The origins of this probably date to the New York Armory Show of 1913, when cubism, expressionism and other forms of modern art made their official American debut, and to the premiere performance in Paris that same year of *Le Sacre du Printemps.* Both events were of the most momentous artistic significance, but this tended to be clouded, then and since, by the great public furors they aroused. It came to be assumed—especially by artists of large ego and small talent—that controversy was the handmaiden of artistic innovation and that it was as intrinsic to art as creativity itself.

Minds capable of making this assumption require no great leap of the imagination to suppose as well that since (a) it is the clear duty of government to finance the arts, (b) it is government's equally clear duty to finance controversy *for its own sake.* That this has no constitutional or statutory foundation is, to such minds, quite beside the point; if art is good and controversy is artistic, then controversy must be funded.

Related to this is the presumption that government is no less obliged to underwrite that art which, whether controversial or not, is merely new. If a single artistic principle can be said to lie at the core of modernism in literature and the arts, it is that the new is to be prized above all and, concomitantly, that the old—or even the recent—is by its very nature to be rejected and/or scorned. Not long ago I read a piece that sneered at critics and readers who are skeptical about "the difficult and the new"; this is the underlying urge of modernism, to create that which is unfamiliar and unprecedented—and to find virtue in it for those qualities alone, quite regardless of its true merits as art.

Thus we have, to take a recent example, the prominent jazz musician Miles Davis, a complex man and a restless artist who soon will be bringing out his autobiography. It is an unpleasant book, but it does speak to the search for the new that dominates modernism whether it be in music or literature or painting or sculpture:

"Bebop was about change, about evolution. It wasn't about standing still and becoming safe. If anybody wants to keep creating they have to be about change. Living is an adventure and a challenge. When people come up to me and ask me to play something like 'My Funny Valentine,' some old thing that I might have done when they were [expletive] this special girl and the music might have made them both feel good, I can understand that. But I tell them to go buy the record. *I'm* not there in that place any longer and I have to live for what is best for me and not what's best for them."

That statement is colored, to be sure, by the peculiarities of Davis's personality and experience, but it speaks to the fundamental assumption that the only worthwhile art is new art. Whether the work he is now doing is superior or inferior to what he did before seems of far less moment to Davis than the indisputable fact that it is different. "New" in his lexicon is implicitly desirable and "old" is no less implicitly contemptible; he speaks dismissively of jazz itself as "becoming the music of the museum."

Other artists in other disciplines no doubt would phrase it in other ways and use other examples, but the essential point is, in the world of contemporary art, universal: What have you done for me lately, baby? An artist or writer may come up with an imaginative idea early in his career, but if he doesn't continue to replace it with new ones each time he appears in public, sooner or later he will be dismissed by the arbiters of taste as retrograde and, therefore, inconsequential.

Not merely that, but artists are expected to accommodate themselves to the pace of the age. Michelangelo might have had four years to paint the ceiling of the Sistine Chapel, and Proust a full decade to write *Remembrance of Things Past*, but such indulgence is frowned upon in our pell-mell world. Thus Davis, whose career goes back a mere four decades, has in that time gone from bop to cool to modern to rock to fusion—each genre getting its brief moment in the sun before giving way to the next phase in the obsessive search for the new.

The problem isn't with the search but with the obsession, and with the conviction that not to innovate is to stagnate. Obviously any healthy culture needs a fairly steady infusion of the new, but it also needs not merely to honor the past but to echo and imitate it—to learn its lessons not only by example but also by repetition. Experimentation and adventure are not the only rewarding artistic experiences; there is much to be said as well for the exploration of the familiar, and for the perceptions and insights it can yield.

If a culture fixated solely on the past is unhealthy—an indisputable proposition—why is one obsessed with the unknown and untried, at the expense of the past, any healthier? When the arts community demands that the public underwrite its incessant quest for the new, why should we accept without challenge not merely that the funding is desirable but that the quest itself is beyond reproach? Hasn't it occurred to anyone that we've been sold a bill of goods, that too much of what we are expected to applaud because it is new is, in fact, merely shallow and meretricious and self-congratulatory?

"Art should be supported by government and protected from politics," the trustees of the Whitney Museum of American Art—a bastion of the new—told the nation last week. Baloney. Art should be supported by those who care about it; if it is, it can fend for itself with no fear of political interference, and it can be just as new and as controversial as it wants.

That's Entertainment

September 25, 1989

It was a familiar scene on the evening news last week. A well-dressed man and woman sat on either side of the screen. Behind them was a bank of monitors, flashing a succession of pictures. In the background could be heard the clatter of a wire-service ticker—not perhaps the most up-to-date device in this age of electronically transmitted information, but still a powerful and evocative symbol of the news.

The only trouble was that this wasn't the news at all, but a commercial, for a Chevrolet dealer in Baltimore, being broadcast during the news. The sale of allegedly marked-down automobiles may or may not be news, but the dealer clearly hoped we would see it as such—hoped, that is, we would fail to distinguish between it and the "real" news it had interrupted, and would therefore view it with a seriousness not ordinarily accorded to the car dealers who howl and clown between segments of the evening's journalism hour.

Thus yet another small step was taken to close the gap between the news and everything else out there in our great wide world of popular culture. News as entertainment, advertising as news, entertainment as news, news as advertising—who can tell who's on first, much less what's on second, when distinctions no longer exist between what is "real" and what is not? America is a fairyland, a funhouse, a penny arcade, a country of make believe where the only certainty is that nothing is certain—that behind the show parading before us is another show, behind it another, with innumerable others retreating ever farther into the distance, their complex meanings and interconnections lost in a fog of obfuscation and deceit.

Consider if you will the latest evidence. Last week we learned that Connie Chung, newly of CBS, is to be the host of a "news" program in which events late and recent will be dramatized; that Tip O'Neill, not long ago second in line of succession to the presidency of the United States, has made a commercial for a chain of motels; that the Knight-Ridder newspapers are considering a redesigned format in which "advertising should be treated as content, with the same power as news to shape readers' feelings about the product," i.e., the newspaper.

How, in this bizarre mélange of news items, are we to determine what is important and what is trivial? For a decade Tip O'Neill, as Speaker of the House of Representatives, certainly was important—if, that is, one is willing to assign genuine importance to anyone in the Congress of the United States—but what is he now, as a shill for American Express and Miller Lite and Hush Puppies and the Trump Shuttle and Quality International? For the motels operated by this last he is to be seen popping, Jack-in-the-box-like, out of a suitcase resting on a bed: "Who says a politician can't save you money?" he asks.

No, I can't see Sam Rayburn doing this, either—or Henry Clay or Nicholas Longworth or Joe Martin or even John Nance Garner. Whatever else the speakership of the House may represent in the public eye, it once stood for something approximating dignity. But where, precisely, is dignity to be found when a former speaker pitches beer and credit cards and pops out of a suitcase?

Believe it or not, apparently it is to be found right there in the commercials. People in politics and government, O'Neill told the *Washington Post* last week, are "happy for me." They think his new eminence as spokesman for shoes and airplanes and computers and banks—and heaven knows what else in the future, as the bucks rise and O'Neill's resistance shrinks—"enhances" the image of people in public life: gives them dignity, if you will.

In a world where news is advertising and advertising is news, doesn't it stand to reason that success in one is interchangeable with success in the other? Tip O'Neill was a major player in the world of news, now he's a celebrity in the world of advertising, and his prominence in the latter lends distinction to his performance in the former; thus runs the logic of the day. Old fogies such as I—and perhaps, dear reader, thou?—may find this vulgar, if not appalling, but to politicians of the television age it is axiomatic: In a culture that knows no shame, how can we expect anyone to find O'Neill's behavior embarrassing?

News is advertising, advertising is news. A former speaker of the House metamorphoses into a pitchman; a car dealer's come-on looks for all the world like the evening news; the egregious Linda Ellerbee and the preposterous Willard Scott—a marriage made in heaven, if ever one was—shuck their garb as "journalists" and emerge, full blown, as mouthpieces for Maxwell House coffee. Yes, a few people in the news business got onto their high horses about the Ellerbee–Scott farrago, but they didn't stay on them for long because no one was paying attention and because the news business—just like the politics business and every other business—is full of people who'd sell their souls for the kind of cash that Ellerbee and Scott are raking in.

In the event we journalists do well to keep the level of our self-righteousness at a respectable low, because journalism has always been inextricably bound to entertainment. For all our pious and self-serving twaddle about the First Amendment, it remains that the press exists to make money and that the easiest way to do so is to entertain, whether by yellow journalism in Hearst's and Pulitzer's newspapers or by sob stories on the evening news. If from time to time we actually provide people with useful, pertinent information that can affect their lives, this is all well and good, but it is, if one cares to take the most skeptical view, incidental to the real business at hand.

So when television tarts up the news by "dramatizing" or "reenacting" it, or when a prominent and influential newspaper chain toys with blurring the line between advertising and editorial copy, perhaps what's going on isn't really quite so revolutionary as retrogrades such as I imagine it to be. Perhaps what we have here is merely the same old opportunism and cynicism, wearing the new clothing of an age in which advertising and entertainment have become as much the news as the news itself. Don't sweat it; go with the flow.

But the opportunism and cynicism do seem rather more blatant, don't they? Probably it's because the stakes are higher and the temptation, accordingly, is greater. The amounts of money being flung around are, by any reasonable standard, unreasonable, so it can hardly be surprising that people are willing to behave shamelessly in hopes of getting their hands on part of the booty. If this means turning the news into entertainment, or advertising into news, who cares? In the great American funhouse, the only thing that counts is the money.

The Philip Morris Bill of Rights

November 13, 1989

Okay. They name football bowl games after sponsors these days. That's great. It's the American way. Go, team! They name golf tournaments after sponsors, too. That's cool. Wouldn't have it any other way. Sink that (ssssh!) putt.

Fork over enough money and you can have any old thing you want, here in the land of the buy-one-get-one-free and the home of the Braves, America's Team. Bowl games, golf tournaments, television shows, senators, evangelists, former presidents, skyscrapers, movie studios: We're running a year-round Washington's Birthday sale, the sellathon to top all sellabrashuns, so come on in, the buyin's great!

Tell that to the good folks at Philip Morris, and they'll just give you a contented smile. Seems a couple of months ago they moseyed on down from Marlboro Country and rounded up a few little dogies in Hicksville, U.S.A., aka Washington, D.C. Ten little dogies, to be precise, name of Bill of Rights, Amendments One through Ten to the U.S. Constitution.

You didn't know the Bill of Rights was up for sale? Must have been one of those private jobs, you know, like the ones at Brooks Brothers and Saks Fifth Avenue and other fine places: Not Announced to the General Public. The Marlboro Man and his podners at Philip Morris just ambled into the National Archives one day back yonder in August, plunked down a few bucks and walked off with the Bill of Rights just as pretty as you please. Not a soul knew a word, 'cepn' the Marlboro Man and the sheep he fleeced there in the li'l ol' Archives building.

But the secret got out last week. Right there on the *ABC Evening News,* right amongst Peter Jennings talking about Berlin and the Virginia election and all those other goings-on. Fade out Jennings, fade in glossy commercials with pictures of great American faces and sounds of great American voices, talking about inalienable rights and liberties and all those things, and then right there at the end an invitation to "join Philip Morris and the National Archives" in celebrating the two hundredth anniversary of the Bill of Rights.

Make that the *Philip Morris Bill of Rights*. Down here in Washington when the boy yells "Call for . . . Phil-ip Mor-rees," he isn't hustling cigarettes, he's pushing freedom of assembly and the right to keep and bear filter tips, not to mention the right to get emphysema or lung cancer any old way you jolly well please. Hustle cigarettes? Heavens no! "We are celebrating the Bill of Rights," a Marlboro Man told the *New York Times.* "It is also a way for us to give the company an identity. We hope people will think better of the company."

Well, how it will play in Peoria remains to be seen, but it's playing like *My Fair Lady* multiplied by *Cats* up there on Mad Ave. According to one Jack Trout of Trout & Ries, described by the *Times* as "a marketing strategy expert," the Philip Morris Bill of Rights ad campaign is "very clever, a way of saying that people have a right to smoke." Trout said: "They have been saying that directly, but this is an indirect, tonier way of saying it. And if they can buy the Bill of Rights for $600,000, that's a deal."

No, man: It's a *steal*. Over two years Philip Morris is going to spend some $60 million on this campaign to improve its "identity," but it got permission to identify itself commercially with the Bill of Rights for a mere $600,000. It didn't just fleece those sheep at Archives; it took them out to the O.K. Corral and carved them into chops and patties. It got the whole Bill of

Rights—"Speedy trial hits the spot,/Ten amendments, that's a lot"—for less than the going price of a sore-armed middle reliever in the bottom half of the American League East.

Yes, you knew Washington was for sale. What you didn't know was just how *cheap*. Privatization is all well and good—who needs national parks, anyway?—but let's at least turn a profit on it. Six hundred thousand bucks gets you, maybe, a studio apartment with a view of the air shaft in a post–World War II papier-mâché apartment building in the east Nineties: no doorman, elevator runs every other day, go to the corner deli if you want room service. That's Manhattan. But in Washington, $600,000 gets you Washington and Jefferson and Adams and "excessive bail shall not be required, nor excessive fines imposed, nor cruel and unusual punishments inflicted."

Makes you wonder if those folks weeping and moaning about the great Bill of Rights sellathon really know what's going on. One of them—would you believe a Naderite?—said the Philip Morris ad "smears the Bill of Rights with the blood of all Americans killed as a result of smoking Marlboro and other Philip Morris cigarettes"; Ralph himself hardly could have said it better, could he? Another—the redoubtable Laurence "Mr. Constitution" Tribe—chimed in, "Some things just should not be for sale."

But, hey, you've missed the point, Larry. Put it this way: "Some things just should not be for sale for $600,000 when you could get $10 mil for them, bottom." According to one of the sheep at Archives, "We think it is very appropriate to stretch the taxpayers' dollars this way," but $600,000 isn't exactly stretching. Hell, it isn't even Hamburger Helper. In Ronald Reagan's Washington—the Gipper may have gone, but it's still His Kind of Town—the most you can expect to get for $600,000 is about a thousand toilet seats.

What they should have done is what Sotheby's does whenever it gets its hands on a nice archive of ornithological watercolors—break the thing up. Instead of selling all ten amendments in one underpriced package, Archives should have peddled them one at a time, for at least $1 million apiece. Why settle for the Philip Morris Bill of Rights when we could have ten sponsors for ten amendments? Admittedly in some cases it might be hard to match sponsor to amendment—"The enumeration of the Constitution, of certain rights, shall not be construed to deny or disparage others retained by the people" doesn't exactly sing, does it?—but that shouldn't stop good old American get up and go.

So after we've gotten rid of the Pampers First Amendment and the Ramada Inn Third Amendment and the Preparation H Sixth Amendment—the client/theme fit may not be so great, but the price is right—do you really think we'll stop there? Of course not. We've got sixteen more amendments to go, and they ought to fetch a pretty penny. The H&R Block Sixteenth Amendment, the Jim Beam Eighteenth Amendment, the Virginia Slims Nineteenth Amendment—why, the possibilities are limitless.

That's just the word: limitless. Once we run out of amendments, why bother to stop? If state legislatures can raise money by establishing lotteries, why can't Congress do the same by passing amendments? Pass one, sell one: If you've got the money, honey, we've got the slime. God bless America.

Speaking of which: The National Anthem ought to bring in at least $50 million. O say can you Sony . . .

Part Three

My Scene

Many Happy Returns

November 2, 1981

For my forty-second birthday, which took place last week, I received a sweater, a pen knife, a picture frame, a casserole dish, a suede hat—and a large plastic bag filled with the severed heads of dead fish. This last, which was delivered to Book World's offices at the *Washington Post*, came in a gold Gucci box (nice touch, that) and was accompanied by a card reading: "From the friends of Kitty Kelley."

Happy Birthday, indeed! Obviously this generous and welcome gift was sent in gratitude for my review in the *Post* of Kelley's new book, *Elizabeth Taylor: The Last Star*, which I had characterized as "a bore" and "a tired, ordinary star bio"; to make the connection absolutely clear, on the other side of the card accompanying the fish heads was a photograph of the luscious (it was taken in 1961) Taylor that had been clumsily doctored so it appeared she was giving me the finger. The friends of Kitty Kelley, like the friends of Eddie Coyle, clearly were out for blood.

So it is with great sorrow that I must tell them—by means of this column, since for some reason they declined to give their names—that none has been shed. Sticks and stones may break my bones, but fish will never hurt me. To be sure, in nearly two decades of writing book reviews and otherwise expressing my opinions in print, I had not previously been assaulted by a sack of fish heads; but I have had my fair share of slings and arrows from outraged and aggrieved authors, and/or their "friends," and I have lived to tell the tale.

My first exposure to severe authorial indignation occurred many years ago when I reviewed the latest novel by a minor writer whose previous books I had liked. My review appeared in a national publication, a copy of which swiftly found its way to the author in California. He decided, at midnight, to telephone me and vent his fury; this he did, refusing to identify himself but leaving absolutely no doubt as to who he was. But inasmuch as his midnight was my three in the morning, and inasmuch as I associate calls at that hour with family illnesses and deaths, I was not unduly grateful to him for moving with such alacrity to inform me with such exactitude as to the nature and extent of his feelings.

But he was not through. He began sending me unsigned letters, in envelopes on which he had carefully written a return address. Why? So that when, fool that I am, I replied, he could allow himself the pleasure of scrawling "REFUSED" across the envelope and having the post office return it to me. (The guy's wit knew no end; he addressed one letter to "Morton Yardley.") These pseudo-anonymous letters were cast in the form of carbon copies of letters to friends of his who, I evidently was to understand, had written to commiserate with him over the injustice to which I had subjected him. One of these read, in part:

"[Yardley] is an infant who cannot discriminate between self and world and who, possessing no sense of history (the one-day memory of a newspaperman), thinks that *my* journalism is 'personal journalism.' . . . Oh dear, how this man wishes he were I, and hates me for being me, and would be me if only he could, and would then hate himself, which he can't do now, being himself."

Then there was the later review, also unfavorable, of another (very) minor writer's new novel. This time a friend of mine happened to attend the author's publication party in New York, where, rubbing elbows and egos with the literati, my friend heard the guest of honor mutter: "I've got a contract out on some guy named Jonathan Yardley." This of course was in jest.

But there was no jest at all, I am reliably informed by a number of people, in the repeated threats by an offended novelist that should he and I ever end up in the same place at the same time, he would clean my clock and punch me out and God knows what else. I had written an especially harsh review of the fellow's especially bloated novel; this appeared seven or eight years ago, and I am told that the author still nurses his grudge. But he missed his golden opportunity. We *were* in the same room at the same time during a booksellers' meeting in Atlanta in 1978. I saw his nametag but he apparently did not see mine. Devoutly believing that discretion is the better part of valor, and knowing full well that this time we were talking sticks and stones and broken bones, not crank calls or fish heads, I kept to my side of the room; he never laid a glove on me.

On and on the stories go. There was the close friendship that dissolved for several years because my friend didn't like what I'd said about his book; that rupture, mercifully, has been healed. There was the time when a colleague began screaming at me in the newsroom where we both worked; the sense of her commotion, to the degree there was any sense to it, was that because of what I had said about her friend's book, I was "hated" by "everyone" in a certain small town in Georgia.

This sort of business does not happen all the time. Screaming colleagues, wee-hours phone calls and fish heads are not the daily lot of the book reviewer. Most authors (and their friends) are sensible people who know by instinct, or have been advised by their publishers, that it is impolitic to assault verbally or otherwise a reviewer who, in the course of duty, has reached an unfavorable judgment of their work. Most authors (and their friends) are sufficiently sophisticated to recognize that writing and publishing a book have built-in risks, one of them being unfavorable reviews.

As it happens I have been on the receiving as well as the giving end of this little folk ritual. I got a few less-than-admiring reviews of a book that I wrote several years ago, and I can report at firsthand two things: The sensation is not pleasant and the urge to retaliate is extreme. But I found that a little bit of cussing in the privacy of my quarters did wonders for my morale; somehow I managed to avoid writing any nasty letters or making any angry phone calls, and I certainly am glad I did.

Perhaps the friends of Kitty Kelley feel otherwise. Perhaps they are convulsed by their wit or impressed by their boldness. But I am of the view that their behavior is even trashier than their friend's book—and that is saying something.

Out of Step

November 23, 1981

The votes are in, the verdict has been reached, and guess what: I lose. A novel that I panned quite emphatically a couple of weeks ago—*A Flag for Sunrise*, by Robert Stone—has by now made the rounds of the reviewers and has been pronounced, with what seems to be unanimity, a work of genius. I am, so far as I can tell, a minority of one.

People writing elsewhere have praised the book extravagantly. John Leonard of the *New York Times* describes *A Flag for Sunrise* as "an exalted thriller" and "the best novel of ideas since Dostoyevski. . . ." Walter Clemons of *Newsweek* writes: "It is now clear that [Stone] is the strongest novelist of the post–Vietnam era. . . . Stone writes as if announcements of the death of the novel had not reached him." *The New Republic* loves the book; so do *Time* and the *Miami Herald* and the *Baltimore Sun*, and heaven knows how many other publications that have not crossed my desk.

Yours truly, by contrast, dismissed the book's political rhetoric as "windy sentimentality" and found the novel as a whole to be "tiresome." Though I would not for a moment withdraw or modify these judgments—if anything they strike me as excessively charitable—I confess to feeling somewhat uncomfortable as I march out of step with the crowd. In the court of literary opinion, going it alone is not always a pleasure.

It all boils down to the question that continually confronts anyone who reviews books or movies or architecture or boxtops: Am I right? To be sure, in matters where *de gustibus* is the prevailing rule, there is no such thing as "right" or "wrong"; what seems a masterpiece to one reader or viewer may seem a disaster to another, and who is to say that either is "right"? Yet in the little world of books, just as in the little world of film or art or anything else, there nonetheless exists a critical consensus; it is this that the reviewer, excepting of course the professional iconoclast, violates with trepidation.

The consensus is shaped by many forces. At certain periods a single powerful critic, or group of critics, speaks with such a magisterial voice that it strongly influences others; in this country there has been no such voice since the death nine years ago of Edmund Wilson. Certain authors accumulate reputations that finally become so imposing as to render them sacrosanct; this happened some time ago to Saul Bellow, and it seems to be happening now to John Updike. There are other pressures as well, arising from within the worlds of publishing and journalism, of which the public is unlikely to be aware.

One of these involves the close relationship that invariably develops between the individual reviewer and the publishing community. In sorting through the staggering volume of new titles brought out each season, the reviewer is assisted by the candor and good judgment of the publicists who represent the publishing houses. Over the years the reviewer comes to trust and like—hell, I *married* one—certain publicists; when one of them approaches him with an enthusiastic recommendation, he has ample reason to view that book positively.

This interacts with the subtler pressure that emanates from the world of journalism: the herd instinct. All the reviewers get the same messages from the same publicists; at the same time these reviewers are in occasional, if irregular, contact with each other—frequent contact if they inhabit the literary precincts of New York City. Word gets around fast: Knopf is high on *A Flag for Sunrise*, Viking thinks *The White Hotel* is a masterpiece, Random House loves *Gorky Park*. For certain books a consensus begins to build well before their actual publication; for reviewers who worry about their standing within the fraternity, going against the flow can seem a risky and unpalatable business.

A further problem for the reviewer is that good books just do not come along all that often. Writing negative reviews, seeming to be a grouch, can be a bore. So when a book arrives that seems considerably better than the run of the mill, when a respected publisher is solidly behind it and there appears a real possibility that a serious writer can enjoy a commercial success, the temptation to leap in with a thundering "major" review can be very strong. I know because I have been there: with *Herzog*, with *The Confessions of Nat Turner*, with *Ragtime*, with *Robert Kennedy and His Times*. Traipsing along with the rest of the crowd, I badly overpraised each of these books; I was concerned that to express a negative opinion, in the face of all these books had going for them, would be "wrong."

It was a long time before I finally realized what I should have known all along, that this is a great disservice to the person who, in the business of reviewing, should matter most: the reader. Too often we forget that reviews are not written for authors or publishers or other reviewers, but for the people who read the newspapers and magazines for which we write. These people presumably read our reviews because they trust our judgment and want our opinions about new books they are thinking about buying. But what repayment of that trust is it to parrot, whether consciously or not, what amounts to a company line? What "service" does that provide for the reader?

I am not saying that the critical hubbub over *A Flag for Sunrise* is necessarily a phenomenon of this sort, though there are certainly elements in the publication and promotion of the novel, and in the novel itself, that made it from the outset a likely candidate for instant, coast-to-coast immortality. My judgment of the book may be hopelessly mistaken; I may be "wrong." But obviously I do not think so, or I would not have written what I did—knowing, as I wrote it, that I was likely to be going against the critical grain.

This, mind you, was no act of courage; I have the courage of a dormouse. It was simply a manifestation of a stubborn skepticism I have developed about literary hype. This skepticism swept over me several years ago, as in a flash of light, while I was reading proofs of a novel called *Falconer*, by John Cheever, a writer whose work I admire. The book had arrived with advance publicity appropriate to the Second Coming; obviously it was going to be praised to the skies and sell like crazy. But after reading it I said to myself, "This is a piece of trendy, pretentious junk." I decided to say the same in my review, though in somewhat more polite language, and I also resolved that I would never again let my concern about the critical consensus prevent me from speaking my mind.

Which is why, having spoken my mind about *A Flag for Sunrise*, I found myself all alone in my own little corner. But I suspect that after a few more people read the novel, I'll have plenty of company there.

Give Me the City Life

January 11, 1982

The other day I had a note from a fellow whom I'd known more than a quarter century ago when we were boys growing up in the Southside Virginia town of Chatham. He told me that after two decades of roving the nation and the world as a journalist, he had returned to Chatham to live—not merely to the town, but to the house in which he had been born. He continues to travel and to write, but with Chatham rather than New York as his base—much, he noted, to "the puzzlement of my New York colleagues."

His letter comes to mind because I have been reading a book (*Return to Main Street,* by Nancy Eberle) that describes a noteworthy reverse migration that began during the 1970s. The twentieth-century pattern of country-come-to-town is doing a turnabout; in considerable numbers, Americans are moving from cities and suburbs to small, rural towns—places just like Chatham. The phenomenon may or may not prove to have long-range ramifications, but it clearly reflects a disenchantment with urban/suburban life and its manifold vexations. The old romantic vision of the country town—Huck and Tom, Penrod and Sam, that little house on the prairie—seems to be regaining its once-powerful place in the national consciousness.

It is not difficult to understand why. Life in the cities is tough, and is almost certain to get tougher as the president and Congress persist in tossing out the urban baby with its bath. If there is to be a dispersal of the population, even a relatively insignificant one, the strain on the cities and the overcrowded conditions within them may be reduced—as also, less beneficially, may be the cities' tax base, since the back-to-the-sticks movement is primarily one of the middle and upper-middle classes. The small town has played a crucial role in the shaping of the American character; that it is undergoing a revival is probably, on balance, good news.

But it is a revival in which I shall not take part. Given the nature of my job, it would be easy enough for me to live in a small town; the weekly trip to Washington that I now make by train from Baltimore could just as easily be made by car, or a combination of car and train, from any one of many lovely little towns within a hundred miles of downtown Washington—I like the looks, for example, of a place in Maryland called Lineboro. But for reasons having something to do with experience and something to do with conviction, I am sticking with the city.

This is not to say that my memories of Chatham are any more painful than most run-of-the-mill childhood memories. By and large they are happy ones. My family moved there in the summer of 1949, when I was nine years old, from a suburb of New York. In a time when the South was still mysterious and alien and *distant* to northerners, the mere act of moving there was in itself thrilling. Into the bargain, my father was taking over the headmastership of a girls' boarding school; I was free to roam its hundreds of acres of farmland and woods, to visit its stables and henhouses and silos, to use its tennis courts and playing fields—and of course to admire, however shyly and from afar, its students.

The town of Chatham was a few minutes' walk down the hill. Then, as now, it had about eighteen hundred residents. There was a grocery store called Mick or Mack; I have never known why. Of the two drugstores, I preferred the one run by Mr. Les Jones, a kind man at whose marble counter an ethereal chocolate ice cream soda was served. There was a five-and-dime, the name of which I can no longer remember, and a Western Auto, where I browsed the bikes and baseball bats. There were substantial edifices in which to worship the God of the Baptists and Methodists; there was a library, and a courthouse that could have been designed by William Faulkner—its habitués probably *were.*

I attended the Chatham Elementary School, known to my parents (and thus to all the family) as the Alimentary School, in imitation of the local accent. One of my classmates, a boy seemingly fated to spend his life in the fifth grade, endeared himself to me forever by having two thumbs on one hand, with a little one growing out of the big one; he was my first exposure to the world of Flannery O'Connor. My friends were boys with good, solid names like Henry Hammer and Billy White and Claude Whitehead; we played baseball and football, invented games in the woods, listened to Al Helfer and Bill Stern on the radio, talked about girls.

I loved Chatham then, and I suppose that I love it still. Each time my wife and I drive south on Route 29, I insist on foregoing the bypass and taking the grand tour, in particular to see the great shade trees and large frame houses that make Main Street the embodiment of everything those two words evoke in the American imagination. The tour takes about ten minutes; it always leaves me awash in memories.

Not all of which are good ones. I hated being sent away to boarding school at the age of eleven; yet the limitations of the Alimentary School virtually commanded that I be. The town was beautiful but narrow, blacks existed in conditions not much better than those of slavery, I knew of only one Catholic family and no Jews, and with my Yankee accent I was a sitting duck for the class bully and other malefactors. There was a harsh, constipated censoriousness in the air; religiosity and self-righteousness went hand in glove in the citadel of fundamentalism.

Most of all I felt an incredible distance from the life of the real world. Obviously I was influenced by my parents, who missed the northeastern world in which both had grown up. But like country boys and girls for generations before me I dreamed my own city dreams—dreams made all the more vivid by radio broadcasts that brought into Virginia evenings the sounds of baseball in St. Louis and dance bands in New Orleans. Quite literally I could hear train whistles in the night; more than anything I wanted to follow them, and soon enough I did.

I am told that in the twenty years since I left it for good, Chatham has made great strides. My parents, who were there at the time, were amazed by the way the town accommodated itself to integration in the early seventies, with grace and a biracial determination to strengthen the community. The social life of the town is reported to be more relaxed, even to the point of tolerating cocktails; in my day, Demon Rum was held to be as wicked as Satan himself. Television and improved roads make the joys (and sorrows) of the larger world more accessible; admittedly the "big city" is still Danville, but who expects perfection?

Still, the lure does not pull me. I admire my friend for returning to Chatham, and I envy him the close connection with his past that the move has given him, but I am a city boy for the duration. In part this is because I am not persuaded that the negative characteristics of small-town life—isolation, enforced intimacy, meddling townspeople—have significantly changed. But in larger part it is simply that I prefer to live in cities.

Yes, I know that two weeks ago a man was murdered just a few houses away from us; that I feel it necessary to lock the house if I take the dog for a ten-minute walk; that I carry a walking stick on nocturnal strolls less for support than for protection—all this in a "safe" neighborhood. And, no, I do not propose to rhapsodize about the symphonies and the museums and the various "cultural advantages" that defenders of cities are so quick to cite; in the age of communications, these amenities are available to just about anybody, anywhere.

I live in the city because: I need frequent, sometimes abrasive contact with the whole rainbow of humanity; nobody thinks I'm weird because I decline to attend the church of my choice; I do not have to drive three hundred miles to find a recording by Tal Farlow or a book by Peter Taylor; big-league baseball is more interesting than high-school football; the newspapers are better, and they publish them every day.

Into the Void

October 31, 1983

For some years it has been fashionable to argue that, the rhythm of American life being such as it is, the real New Year begins not on the first day of January but on the day after Labor Day, and that this year has two seasons; they are called School and Vacation. This is a plausible notion, and an appealing one, and my inclination has been to go along with it. Of late, though, I have been giving it sober reflection, and have reluctantly concluded that the truth lies elsewhere.

This is because the wrenching experience of the past two weeks has convinced me that the true American New Year begins on the first Monday in April and is divided into two seasons, or parts, so astonishingly dissimilar as to numb the mind. These seasons are known as Baseball and The Void, or, in certain less interesting circles, as Summer and Winter. In the current year—the Year of the Bird—it has been two weeks since Baseball came to its sudden and wholly gratifying conclusion with my Baltimore Orioles' victory in the World Series. Unfortunately, we were able to enjoy this gratification for only an instant, since with the final postgame interview we were plunged immediately into the outer darkness called The Void.

There are many ways to describe the difference between Baseball and The Void; they were nicely summarized the other day by a friend of mine who, contemplating the long, bleak, dolorous times ahead, poignantly asked, "But what do we do at night?" That indeed is the question. During Baseball it hardly ever has to be asked; except on the occasional rainout or off day, at night one goes to the game, either in person or by means of the radio. But during The Void there are no games to attend and thus there is nothing—or nothing important—to do. During The Void we are left entirely to our own resources, with consequences that occasionally are rewarding but often are merely disorienting.

To be sure, during The Void it is possible to make the acquaintance of certain amenities that do tend, during Baseball, to get lost in the shuffle between Fenway and Anaheim. Among these are music, books, movies, the theater, restaurants and even (!) work. Were it not for The Void I might never have chanced upon Cesar Franck's stirring Sonata for Violin and Piano, or Ross Thomas's delicious novel, *Missionary Stew,* or the movie *Atlantic City,* or the play *The Dining Room,* or the Imperial Crab at Thompson's Sea Girt House—and without these, admit it I must, life would be rather less interesting than, with them, it is.

It is also true that during the endless days of The Void it is possible to undertake the arrangement of that peculiar institution known as "social life." During Baseball, the only permissible "social life" involves sitting next to a person, preferably a person with whom one is on speaking terms, in the ballpark; if a person wishes to see one "socially" and does not appreciate the pleasures of the ballpark, that person's wishes cannot be accommodated. Thus it was that during the recently ended Baseball, I had no choice except to fend off invitations issued by an otherwise charming acquaintance who, being of the British faith, had not the slightest understanding of the "social" subtleties of Baseball. Now that we are in The Void it will be possible to see this gentleman again, and I look forward to our meetings as though they were glowing candles in the long, chill darkness.

It is furthermore true, to give the devil his due, that during The Void there are certain liberating elements toward which gratitude must be directed, however reluctantly. It is not necessary, during The Void, to grope for the telephone in the early morning hours in order to dial up the number that gives recorded scores from the West Coast; not having to discharge this obligation at the crack of dawn is, I must acknowledge, a relief. It is also a relief—well, at least it's a change—to be able to undertake an activity at 7:35 of an evening without fulfilling the conflicting obligation to turn on the radio and enter that three-hour period of apprehension and agony known as a "game." It is a relief—sorry about that, guys—to be able to get through the sports pages in a couple of minutes and thus have ample time for the contemplation of James Watt, Margaret Thatcher, Johnny Carson and other such personages before setting about the day's affairs.

In fact, so long as confession is the order of the day, let it be said that during The Void it is possible to travel—to travel as freely as a bird, with no encumbrances imposed by the scheduling department of the American League. Not merely is it possible to get up and go at any old moment, with nary a thought for the home-and-away rotation, but it is also possible to get up and go to any old place, even one that doesn't have a radio station. It is possible to arrive at some distant and alluring place and to read its newspapers without cursing them for failing to elucidate all matters Baltimorean to a length of several thousand words and eighty-seven inches of statistics.

Okay: It had just as well be acknowledged that during The Void there is time to renegotiate diplomatic relations with the rest of the world, a world that quite simply disappears during Baseball. This is a world that includes the likes of dentists, art-museum guides, appliance repairmen, symphony conductors, loan officers, butchers, insurance adjusters, professors, upholsterers, cabinetmakers, barristers, stand-up comedians, bosses—these and all the others who vanish into the ether at the beginning of Baseball, which of course occurs on that great national holiday called Opening Day.

The Void is the season when one deals with these people, some of whom are quite civilized. There are, by my count, a mere 154 days remaining in this season of The Void in this Year of the Bird, which is to say a mere 154 days in which to take care of all the year's trivial necessities before the arrival of that most necessary triviality, Baseball.

So what I want to know is this: If The Void offers so much pleasure and productivity as, alas, it seems to, why do I spend all six months of it wishing it was over?

Good Old Golden Rule Days

May 19, 1986

On a warm, sunny day in North Carolina last week, James Barrett Yardley was awarded—to the delight and astonishment of his mother, father, stepmother, brother, girlfriend and (need it be said?) teachers—the degree of bachelor of arts. His cynical old father, sitting in the south stands at Kenan Stadium in Chapel Hill, had to wage a manly battle to keep from breaking down and blubbering like a baby.

No doubt both the spectacle and the catharsis will be equally overpowering three years hence, when brother Bill receives the same degree in the same place, but there can be no getting around it: The graduation from college of your eldest child is an event guaranteed to reduce you to the physical and emotional condition of Silly Putty. That is all the more so when, as was the case with me last week, the child's graduation coincides with the twenty-fifth anniversary of your own departure from the same institution; it is about as much overload as a middle-class American's emotions can bear.

Had it not been for Jim's commencement, I probably would have passed over my own reunion, both because of shyness in crowds and because my close friends were not concentrated in my own class, but scattered among many. So I have my son to thank for this, as for so many other things: By luring me down to Chapel Hill, he presented me not merely with the indescribable pleasure of being witness to his own passage into adult life, but with the opportunity to reconnect myself to my own undergraduate years.

The University of North Carolina does many things well—after last week, I'd say graduation ceremonies in particular—but alumni reunions do not seem to be among them. Perhaps this is true of most large state universities, whose graduating classes are too big to have strong identities and loyalties; I was told by a classmate's husband, an alumnus of an Ivy League school, that his university would be humiliated if it could do no better than the 10 percent turnout that the U.N.C. Class of 1961 produced, abetted by a halfhearted recruiting effort by the alumni office. Hundreds weren't there who should have been, and they were missed.

Yet in the end none of that really mattered. If many people I'd wanted to see didn't make it, many others did; and, as apparently happens routinely at class reunions, a number of classmates previously little known to me turned out to be entirely interesting and delightful people. To be sure, the experience of seeing one's classmates for the first time in a quarter century is not without its unsettling aspects: the graying hair, the expanded waistlines, the wrinkles and crinkles—are these really the people I went to school with? But let he who is without sin cast the first stone; at least a dozen people asked where on earth all my hair had gone.

When we weren't casting nervous eyes at one another's deteriorating physiques, we were moaning about how the world in general, and Chapel Hill in particular, had gone to hell in a handbasket. This seems to be as much a part of the silver-reunion ritual as the execrable food at the class banquet. In the case of Chapel Hill, though, the complaints were not without justification. The central campus of the first state university is still, in my judgment, about as beautiful as any place on earth, but travel a mile or two from the Old Well and you're in a land utterly foreign to the Class of '61: Condo City, jammed with shopping centers and strip developments and high-rise dormitories and roads suffering from terminal gridlock. Like other once-small communities famed for their beauty and charm, Chapel Hill has gotten too popular for its own good.

Chapel Hill was once a village; our class is one of the last to have known it as such, and I guess we must be grateful that we at least have the memory. Yet as is almost always the case in human affairs, loss is counterbalanced by gain. If many good things the Class of '61 remembers are gone, some bad ones are gone as well. Most specifically, like other major universities in the South—and the rest of the country, for that matter—the University of North Carolina is no longer the captive of antiquated, debilitating social and cultural customs. This is to say that in one crucial respect, the university from which my son graduated is radically different from, and improved upon, the one from which I did: It is open to every student who can qualify for admission.

Among the senior-class photographs in the 1961 *Yackety Yack*—the egregious name with which U.N.C. yearbooks are saddled—you will find only one black face; but in the crowd of students who marched joyfully across Kenan Stadium's playing field last Sunday, there were more black faces than even the nimblest mathematician could have counted. Many significant changes have occurred in American higher education in the past quarter century, many of them much to its detriment, but this one is as heartening as it is important. In 1961 public higher education was to all intents and purposes separate and unequal; though most schools are still predominantly black or predominantly white, the old barriers have long since fallen.

The result is that institutions long prideful of their traditions of academic freedom now offer genuine freedom of opportunity as well. For everyone concerned, this makes them better places: more open, more diverse, more representative of the society that supports them. The university in which my sons have studied is vastly more heterogeneous than the one I attended, and for that reason if no other it doubtless has taught them more—just as it has provided a richer education for their black schoolmates, whose mothers and fathers were expected to attend black-only colleges. Say all you will about the deleterious changes that have affected higher education since 1961, but in this respect there has been nothing but progress, pure and simple.

For that reason the Class of 1986, when it gathers in Chapel Hill twenty-five years from now, will look quite unlike the Class of 1961 as it assembled last week. But in one respect, the two classes are exactly the same: Their members are graduates of a university to which they are bound for life and which shaped their lives in more ways than they will ever know. The same is true at campuses all across the nation, in this month of graduations and reunions. The young depart in joy and the old return in gratitude, to the place that, through the deep loyalty it exacts, unites them all. Which is why Jim and I have a date to meet again in Chapel Hill: in May 2011.

Mr. Reston

August 17, 1987

Word of James Barrett Reston's retirement from daily journalism reached me two and a half weeks ago at a motel on Cape Cod. It came by way of a handsome tribute to Mr. Reston—pardon the deviation from *Washington Post* style, but calling him "Reston" is inconceivable to me—on ABC's evening news broadcast. It was, I assumed, the first shot in what would become a fusillade of celebration and praise, one that would render anything I might have to say upon my return from vacation belated, superfluous and redundant.

So much for my prognosticatory powers. What follows is certainly belated and possibly superfluous, but it is scarcely redundant. ABC's portrait of Mr. Reston was followed not by a chorus of salutation but by a silence so vast that it seemed to encompass the entire business of journalism. In no newspaper or magazine that I have seen this month has there been more than perfunctory mention of Mr. Reston's reduced responsibilities at the *New York Times;* to the embarrassment of all journalists, due tribute has not been paid.

It would be comforting and convenient to chalk this off to journalism's preoccupation with the Iran-contra hearings and other such amusements, but that would be an excuse rather than an explanation. The lamentable fact is that the business to which he brought so much honor and distinction had neglected Mr. Reston by the hour of his retirement; the telling irony is that Mr. Reston, for all his working life a believer in the lessons of history, is himself a victim of American journalism's indifference to history, its own included.

Thus it is that I find myself not in the awkward position of adding a footnote to what others have already said, but in the even more uncomfortable one of wanting to say all the things that have gone unsaid. This I cannot hope to do, for in a career of nearly half a century Mr. Reston did and wrote so much that no mere newspaper column can adequately summarize or assess it. Instead I should like to put a personal note on the public record, and to offer a comment or two about why Mr. Reston seems to me not merely the leading journalist of his generation, but an example to younger journalists that we ignore at our own peril.

I first met Mr. Reston in the late winter of 1961; I was a senior at the University of North Carolina, where he had come to deliver a speech and meet with students. A series of wholly improbable events ensued, the final result of which was that two weeks after graduation I reported for work at the Washington bureau of the *New York Times.* Mr. Reston, who was then chief of that bureau as well as a thrice-weekly columnist, had been persuaded by his friend Felix Frankfurter that a prominent journalist, like a Supreme Court justice, should have a clerk; thanks to extraordinary good luck, the position was mine.

To say that I was overwhelmed by my good fortune scarcely hints at the truth. Not merely was Mr. Reston then the most celebrated and respected journalist in the country, but he presided over a bureau that overflowed with talent. Arthur Krock was a looming, intimidating presence—his role as waterboy to Joe Kennedy was as yet unrevealed—and so too were the older journalists whom he had hired during his own tenure as chief of the *Times'* Washington satrapy. But to me the most impressive reporters were those whom Mr. Reston had brought on: Tom Wicker, Anthony Lewis, Marjorie Hunter, Max Frankel, David Halberstam, Richard Mooney, Russell Baker—the leaders-to-be of journalism's next generation.

The collective presence of these people in one rather small

office in Washington was tribute not merely to their own abilities but even more to Mr. Reston's sympathy for younger journalists and his determination to bring the best of them into his bureau. To his twenty-one-year-old clerk they seemed stars from another planet, as of course he did too; over a quarter century I have never quite lost the awe I felt at being permitted to spend a year in such company, nor have I satisfactorily repaid the great debt I owe to Mr. Reston for letting me begin my career in such auspicious circumstances.

I gained many things from that year with Mr. Reston, but nothing more than the conviction that journalism should be a serious business for serious people. That conviction is terribly difficult to sustain in this new age of celebrity journalists and "personal" journalism, but it is a belief worth fighting to hold on to. Both as bureau chief and as columnist, Mr. Reston knew that the story was more important than the storyteller, and that the sensation of the scoop was trivial by comparison with the dogged pursuit of the truth. Not always successfully, I have tried to conduct my own career on the assumption that he was right.

Mr. Reston was and remains an old-fashioned man, a believer in institutions—marriage and the *New York Times*, to name two he especially reveres—and in the principles on which they are founded. The not surprising result is that when journalism started to get trendy, around the late 1960s, it became fashionable in certain circles to mock him as a defender of the establishment, as a sentimental apologist for a corrupt political system—as, in his own words, a "stick-in-the-mud optimist." Among many of his fellow journalists, if not among his millions of devoted readers, he fell out of favor.

This was not entirely without reason. Over the last decade Mr. Reston's columns became more oracular than reportorial, which is to say that a strength was replaced by a shortcoming. Mr. Reston never became, as many admirers had thought he would, "the next Lippmann," because he had neither the training nor a true gift for philosophical reflection. He was, instead, a reporter and an analyst, and no one in his time was better than he at either. Which is to say that he was the first and only Reston, and that is quite enough distinction for anyone to claim.

So before his fellow journalists rush to inter him with yesterday's news, they'd do well to reflect upon the professional standards to which he adhered: the intense, self-effacing loyalty to the institution for which he worked; the belief that obligations to one's country and one's moral convictions take precedence over journalistic ambitions; the ability to see the human side of public events, and to keep always in mind that the people with whom he worked were private individuals whose lives involved more than the workplace and the competition for success.

In any assessment of James Reston, this last quality may well be the one his colleagues and competitors most cherish. He was a tough, resourceful reporter, and under the pressure of a deadline or a big story he occasionally seemed distant and preoccupied, but somehow he managed to remember that he was dealing with people and to treat them accordingly; he knew how to be kind, and he did not hesitate to use that knowledge. He offered his friendship openly and maintained it steadfastly; the knowledge that he is there should I need his help or counsel has been a gift beyond measure, more to be treasured even than the incomparable professional example he set.

A Visit from G. Reaper

August 21, 1989

In the immortal and incontrovertible words of Thomas W. "Fats" Waller: One never knows, do one? A day last week that began in the bright sunlight of youth ended, entirely unexpectedly, in the gloomy shadows of age—or, as we prefer to call it now, "modern maturity." In the equally immortal and equally incontrovertible words of Joe Jacobs: I should of stood in bed.

It all started with Woodstock. Yes, Woodstock. Unless you had your radio and television turned off, and your newspaper and magazine subscriptions canceled, you know that last week was Woodstock Week. Everywhere you looked there were stories about Woodstock, movies about Woodstock, radio programs about Woodstock—two decades after the fact, the high water mark of Flower Power was in the news, and every pundit was having his say.

So naturally this pundit began cranking up the gears, pouring Woodstock into the fuel tank of what passes for his imagination and trying to get the old machine rolling. Ah, Woodstock! In August of 1969, when the multitudes assembled in that sheep meadow or cow pasture or whatever it was—not to mention wherever it was, because it certainly wasn't the little town of Woodstock—I was twenty-nine years old and cursing my bad luck not to be there: loud music, pouring rain, rivers of bad California wine, women running around with their shirts off—it sounded like heaven on earth, and there I was several hundred miles to the south, trapped in the suffocation of suburbia.

So when the movie came out a year later I was first in line. I wrote ecstatically about it for the newspaper by which I was then employed—you'll be glad to hear that the clipping somehow has vanished from my files—and bought the three-record album, which I played until the grooves wore away. Country Joe and the Fish, Richie Havens, Grace Slick, Joe Cocker—like, man, it was the dawning of the Age of Aquarius, and if a record album was as close as I could get, well, that's where I wanted to be.

So last week I went looking for *Woodstock*, figuring to plug myself back in to some of that sixties magic. Of course the album had disappeared, probably swallowed up by the same black hole that had dispatched my ancient column about the wonders and glories of Woodstock. Too bad, I thought, but not all *that* bad, because when you get right down to it the music at Woodstock really was pretty dreary, and the mud and the rain were bummers, and speaking of bummers: What about the sixties? Were they flowers and peace and love or were they—like Woodstock itself—just another chapter in the story of American commerce?

These and other dark thoughts were coursing, or stumbling, through my mind on Wednesday morning when the doorbell rang. It was the mailman, toting his daily load of bills and books. He emptied his bag, wished me a good day, and went his way.

Good day, indeed! That wasn't any mailman, that was Pandora, and right there at the top of the box was the bad news: My very own envelope, personally addressed by "CAR-RT SORT ** CR01," containing my "MEMBERSHIP ACCEPTANCE CERTIFICATE," accompanied by my very own personal letter ("Dear J. Yardley . . .") from Horace B. Deets, Executive Director.

Of what, you ask? Not, alas, of the Baseball Hall of Fame or the Wine and Cheese Society or even the Benevolent and Protective Order of Newspaper Columnists. No, Horace B. Deets is executive director of the You Can't Go Home to Woodstock Again Club, also known as the American Association of Retired Persons. Horace B. Deets has "more than 28 million young (that's me, Horace B. Deets) and putting it into the over-padded Social Security checks of the overprivileged middle-class old. Maybe the day will come when I'm ready to sign on with "the biggest citizens group in America"—i.e., the biggest special-interest group—but until it does, count me out, take me off your mailing list, forget I exist.

No sir, J. Yardley is my name and forever young is my game. Help yourself to *Modern Maturity;* me, I'm signing up for *Jack and Jill* and *My Weekly Reader* and *Seventeen.* Tomorrow I'm getting a skateboard, and next week I'm taking Nintendo classes. I may need six years to grow one, but I aim to have a little pigtail down the back of my neck and to learn what a Bon Jovi is; I'd thought it was a cleansing powder, but I think I was wrong. I'm going to start saying "like" a lot, and "wow," and "you know," and I'll wear rings on my fingers and Swatches on my toes.

Mainly, though, I'll think about Woodstock a lot. It may make for a pretty odd spectacle—a middle-aged bald man with wattles and mottles, sitting there ruminating about Jimi Hendrix and Janis Joplin—but to me it looks like a ticket to the Fountain of Youth. And if what's pouring out of that fountain is bad California wine, well, what I say is, drink up!

people" in his organization and now, J. Yardley, Horace B. Deets wants *you.*

As they say in the comics: Eek! He may call himself Horace B. Deets, but you know, J. Yardley, that his real name is G. Reaper. What on earth was he doing knocking on your door? After all, you were thinking thoughts about Woodstock—old fogy thoughts, to be sure, but that's neither here nor there—and you were wearing raggedy Bermuda shorts and (I swear!) a T-shirt from the Gap, and into the bargain you were two full months shy of your fiftieth birthday: And as Horace B. Deets himself says: "IMPORTANT: YOU MUST BE 50 OR OVER."

Or, as he says, a few lines later, "ACCEPTANCE GUARANTEED IF YOU'RE 50 OR OVER." So why are you coming after me, Horace B. Deets, aka G. Reaper, you with your siren song of a subscription to *Modern Maturity* magazine and "Medicare assistance" and "reasonably priced prescription drugs and vitamins" and counsel from the National Gerontology Research Center? You've got the wrong guy, Horace B. Deets: I'm a kid, I wear Gap shirts and grubby shorts and I think about Woodstock *all the time.* So what if Woodstock was twenty years ago? It's the thought that counts, isn't it?

Okay, I'll admit that the other day I was standing in front of a multiple mirror and that the mirror, in its multiplicity (duplicity?), revealed an assortment of wattles and mottles previously unknown to me. I shouldn't have looked; what you don't know can't hurt you. But wattles and mottles are one thing, a lifetime subscription to *Modern Maturity* quite another: A few minutes of what Horace B. Deets calls the "lively reading" in that magazine and the grave suddenly seems a happy alternative.

So thanks a lot, Horace B. Deets, but no thanks. You may want to be my "voice in Washington," for a mere five dollars a year, but you and I aren't speaking the same language. Not merely do you want to cart me off into the sunset years two decades before my time, but you want to use my five dollars to lobby for taking money out of the paychecks of the wage-earning

About the Author

JONATHAN YARDLEY has been the book critic and a columnist for the *Washington Post* since 1981. Previously he worked for the *New York Times*, the *Greensboro Daily News*, the *Miami Herald* and the *Washington Star*. He is the author of *Ring: A Biography of Ring Lardner* and *Our Kind of People: The Story of an American Family*, as well as a contributor to *The Ultimate Baseball Book* and *Family Portraits*. In 1968 he was awarded a Nieman Fellowship in Journalism at Harvard University, and in 1981 he won the Pulitzer Prize for distinguished criticism. He lives in Baltimore with his wife, Susan Hartt Yardley.